THE L... *the gro*... *paperbo*... *the worl*... *original intro*... *a chronology of the poet's career, a bibliography and notes on the poetry.*

WILLIAM JAY SMITH *has taught at Washington University, Columbia University and is now Poet in Residence at Williams College. He is the author of "Poems" (1947), "Celebration at Dark" (1950), "Poems 1947–1957" (1957), and four collections of children's poems. Well known as the translator of "Poems of a Multimillionaire" by Valery Larbaud and "Selected Writings of Jules Laforgue," Mr. Smith has been elected to the Vermont House of Representatives.*

RICHARD WILBUR, *the General Editor, has won the Pulitzer Prize, the National Book Award, and the Millay Prize, all three in 1957 for his book of poems, "Things of This World." He has recently published a new volume of poetry, "Advice to a Prophet." He has held a Guggenheim Fellowship and is a member of the National Institute of Arts and Letters. He is now Professor of English at Wesleyan University.*

The Laurel Poetry Series
General Editor, Richard Wilbur

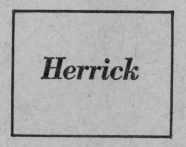

Herrick

Selected, with an introduction
and notes, by William Jay Smith

Published by
DELL PUBLISHING CO., INC.
750 Third Avenue
New York 17, N.Y.

Laurel ® TM 674623, Dell Publishing Co., Inc.

Designed by Alvin Eisenman

Cover drawing by Richard Powers

First printing: August, 1962

Printed in U.S.A.

Contents

Introduction, 13
Bibliography, 27
Chronology, 29

HESPERIDES

The Argument of his Book, 31
When he would have his verses read, 31
The Parliament of Roses to Julia, 32
To his Mistresses, 32
Soft Musick, 32
The shooe tying, 33
Why Flowers change colour, 33
The Vine, 33
Love's play at Push-pin, 34
Cherrie-ripe, 34
To his Mistresses, 34
His request to Julia, 35
All things decay and die, 35
TO THE KING, Upon his comming with his Army into the
      West, 35
To the reverend shade of his religious Father, 36
Delight in Disorder, 36
To Dean-bourn, a rude River in Devon, by which some-
      times he lived, 37
His Cavalier, 37
To Criticks, 37
Upon Blanch, 38
Barly-Break: or, Last in Hell, 38
A Country life, 38

To the Painter, to draw him a Picture, 42

Upon Cuffe. Epig., 42

The frozen Zone: or, Julia disdainfull, 42

An Epitaph upon a child, 43

Upon Scobble. Epig., 43

His fare-well to Sack, 43

The Custard, 45

The suspition upon his over-much familiarity with a
     Gentlewoman, 45

Single life most secure, 46

Some comfort in calamity, 46

The Vision, 46

Love me little, love me long, 47

Upon Strut, 47

TO THE KING, To cure the Evill, 47

Upon Jollies wife, 48

To a Gentlewoman, objecting to him his gray haires, 48

Upon a black Twist, rounding the Arme of the Countesse
     of Carlile, 49

A Ring presented to Julia, 49

Julia's Petticoat, 50

Corinna's going a Maying, 51

Upon Batt, 53

An Ode to Master Endymion Porter, upon his Brothers
     death, 53

To his dying Brother, Master William Herrick, 54

How Lillies came white, 54

On Gelli-flowers begotten, 55

The Lilly in a Christal, 55

Upon some women, 57

The Welcome to Sack, 57

Impossibilities to his friend, 60

Upon Luggs. Epig., 60

Upon Gubbs. Epig., 60

To live merrily, and to trust to Good Verses, 60

To the Fever, not to trouble Julia, 62

To Violets, 63

Upon Bunce. Epig., 63
To the Virgins, to make much of Time, 63
His Poetrie his Pillar, 64
Safety on the Shore, 65
To the Lark, 65
A Meditation for his Mistresse, 66
Lyrick for Legacies, 66
Great boast, small rost, 67
The Fairie Temple: or Oberons Chappell, 67
To Musique, to becalme his Fever, 71
No Lock against Letcherie, 72
Neglect, 72
Upon himselfe, 72
Upon Sudds a Laundresse, 73
To his Booke, 73
Upon a crooked Maid, 73
Draw Gloves, 73
The Hock-cart, *or* Harvest home, 73
Not to love, 75
How Roses came red, 75
Upon Groynes. Epig., 76
To the Willow-tree, 76
The Poets good wisbes for the most hopefull and hand-
    some Prince, the Duke of Yorke, 77
More potent, lesse peccant, 77
To Meddowes, 77
A Nuptiall Song, or Epithalamie, on Sir Clipseby Crew
    and his Lady, 78
The silken Snake, 83
Upon Shark. Epig., 83
Oberons Feast, 83
Upon a child that dyed, 85
To Daffadills, 85
The Christian Militant, 85
His embalming to Julia, 86
The Kisse. A Dialogue, 86
To Larr, 87

The departure of the good Dæmon, 87
Upon his Julia, 88
To my ill Reader, 88
Her Bed, 88
Her Legs, 88
Long and Lazie, 89
Chop-Cherry, 89
His Lachrimæ or Mirth, turn'd to mourning, 89
Upon his kinswoman Mistris Elizabeth Herrick, 90
To his Valentine, on S. Valentines day, 90
Upon M. Ben. Johnson. Epig., 90
To his Nephew, to be prosperous in his art of Painting, 91
Upon Eeles. Epig., 91
The Dreame, 91
Clothes do but cheat and cousen us, 92
To Dianeme, 92
The mad Maids song, 92
Upon Julia's unlacing her self, 93
The Poet loves a Mistresse, but not to marry, 94
Observation, 94
Putrefaction, 94
To Daisies, not to shut so soone, 95
Oberons Palace, 95
To Oenone, 98
An Epitaph upon a Virgin, 99
To Jealousie, 99
Upon himself, 99
To Blossoms, 100
Upon his departure hence, 100
Upon his eye-sight failing him, 101
To a Bed of Tulips, 101
To the Water Nymphs, drinking at the Fountain, 102
Upon a Flie, 102
To Julia, 103
To the right Honourable Edward Earle of Dorset, 103
Upon Love, 103
His Winding-sheet, 104

To Phillis to love, and live with him, 105
Upon her feet, 106
Ill Government, 107
Anacreontike, 107
An Ode to Sir Clipsebie Crew, 107
To his Tomb-maker, 108
His content in the Country, 108
Art above Nature, to Julia, 109
Upon the losse of his Finger, 110
Upon Irene, 110
The Apparition of his Mistresse calling him
    to Elizium, 110
The Primrose, 112
No luck in Love, 112
A charme, or an allay for Love, 113
The Head-ake, 113
To his Booke, 113
His Prayer to Ben. Johnson, 113
The bad season makes the Poet sad, 114
The Night-piece, to Julia, 114
Glorie, 115
Poets, 115
No despight to the dead, 115
The Coblers Catch, 115
The Beggar to Mab, the Fairie Queen, 116
The Hag, 116
The Country Life, 117
To Electra, 119
To Fortune, 120
Upon his Verses, 120
The Funerall Rites of the Rose, 120
The May-pole, 121
Men mind no state in sicknesse, 121
The Bracelet of Pearle: to Silvia, 122
His returne to London, 122
Not every day fit for Verse, 123
Proof to no purpose, 123

His Grange, or private wealth, 124

Up tailes all, 125

A Ternarie of littles, upon a pipkin of Jellie
     sent to a Lady, 125

The Smell of the Sacrifice, 126

Lovers how they come and part, 126

The Wake, 126

A Conjuration, to Electra, 127

A Hymne to Bacchus, 128

Upon Julia's Clothes, 129

Upon Prew his Maid, 129

The Amber Bead, 129

The Transfiguration, 129

Upon Love, 130

No difference i'th'dark, 130

The Body, 130

Kisses Loathsome, 130

Charmes, 131

The Ceremonies for Candlemasse day, 131

Upon Ben. Johnson, 131

An Ode for him, 131

The present time best pleaseth, 132

Cloathes, are conspirators, 132

Upon Julia's washing her self in the river, 132

Upon Blisse, 133

On Himselfe, 133

Anacreontike, 133

Anacrontick Verse, 134

Parcell-gil't-Poetry, 134

Upon Love, by way of question and answer, 135

The Vision, 135

Comfort to a youth that had lost his Love, 136

Peace not Permanent, 136

His desire, 136

The Tinkers Song, 137

Another on Love, 137

To his Girles who would have him sportfull, 137

On himselfe, 138
Upon Spur, 138
The Hagg, 138
To his Booke, 139
On Himselfe, 139
The pillar of Fame, 140

HIS NOBLE NUMBERS

His Letanie, to the Holy Spirit, 141
A Thanksgiving to God, for his House, 142
To his Conscience, 144
Another Grace for a Child, 144
A Christmas Caroll, sung to the King in the
      Presence at White-Hall, 145
The Widdowes teares: of, Dirge or Dorcas, 146
The white Island: or place of the Blest, 148
His Meditation upon Death, 149
This Crosse-Tree, 151

Notes, 152

Introduction

I

After suffering complete neglect during the entire eighteenth century, Robert Herrick regained his place in the pantheon of English lyric poets. The nineteenth-century estimate of him seems best summarized by Swinburne, who said that "he is and will probably be always the first in rank and station of English song-writers. . . . Elegy or litany, epicede or epithalamium, his work is always a song-writer's; nothing more, but nothing less, than the work of the greatest song-writer—as surely as Shakespeare is the greatest dramatist—ever born of English race." Herrick knew what he could do, said Swinburne, "a rare and invaluable gift," and having been born a blackbird or a thrush, he did not "take himself (or try) to be a nightingale." John Masefield said also in 1906 that perhaps no English poet has shown "a more complete mastery of the art of delicate writing." But Masefield is careful to define Herrick's limitations: "He is never quite 'a man of this world.' He creates, or adopts, a fictitious world, which one has to accept in accepting him. The things of that world are the dainty and luxurious things, which are pleasant to catalogue in dainty verses. The people of that world are either Watteau shepherds or Fragonard nymphs; and in either case they are unreal, but adorable, playthings. . . . He was not a lover of human beings. He was a lover of parts, of points, of separate qualities or beauties." It is this very pleasantness and prettiness that has led in our time not only to a popular acceptance of Herrick but also to a different sort of neglect.

The qualities that make Herrick so delightful a lyricist

also seem to make him one of the major English poets least fitted for careful study and critical evaluation. Modern scholars have devoted themselves to the background and sources of his poems, and only recently we have had the first complete critical edition of his work. But critics have paid him little attention for the simple reason that his poems present few difficulties. What is there to discuss or analyze in a poet who writes so simply, so delicately, and so directly? Undergraduates today like him and read him in the same uncritical way that they do a modern poet like E. E. Cummings; and their professors are apt to let them do so and to devote their major efforts of analysis and explication to the more difficult and meatier work of a poet like Donne. In his poem "False Nightmare," Allen Tate in the "sleep-awakened mind" assigns these words to Walt Whitman:

> "I give the yawp barbaric
> Of piety and pelf
> (Who now reads Herrick?)..."

The answer is, "Not many," if we mean something more than superficial reading.

"Herrick was a real gentleman, sir," said a Southern student to his professor, "a man like that could never use a dirty word." Herrick did use many, as the student would have discovered had he examined the complete poems. But a gentleman he was, and a gentle man. *Two Gentle Men,* Miss Marchette Chute entitles a recent study of the lives of George Herbert and Robert Herrick. But since so little is known of Herrick's life, Miss Chute has had to limit herself to a detailed discussion of background and to a portrait of the poet as he emerges from his poetry. With her conclusion that for "all its oddities and its many failures, *Hesperides* is one of the most beautiful books ever written" one must agree, but the reasons for that particular beauty are difficult to define. Herrick's uniqueness appears somehow to escape us. What was it that he alone among English poets was able to do?

Of delicacy it is always difficult to speak, and because Herrick is so modest a poet, and so clear about what he is doing, a weighty treatment will inevitably appear to labor the obvious. The last words of "The Country Life" are *cætera desunt*—"the rest is wanting"; and this is true of many of Herrick's poems. Because he is a master of understatement, he knows what to omit. What is only hinted at or suggested is often the most important part of the poem. Herrick chooses always a small frame in which to work. It best fits his "little note," and "little" is one of his favorite adjectives. Herrick is a perfect miniaturist; nothing is too small for him to notice or too great to reduce in size. Lafcadio Hearn found him of all English poets closest in spirit to the Japanese, not only because of his love of short and delicate verse forms, but for his perceptions as well. He is a supreme water-colorist, and with his quick brush-strokes he suggests the *haiku* and the *tanka* centuries before they were known in English. Herrick's world is a small world, depicted with a spring freshness and an early-morning shimmer.

The principal inhabitants of this world are girls and flowers, and together they act out over and over a strange series of little dramas, changing one into the other at will. What is the sense of all these playthings, and this play? No poet has ever presented his readers with such a bevy of beauties. They appear separately and together, moving about the alcove like succubi, ever ready to serve their master. Primping and pouting, they always seem prepared at a moment's notice for whatever game their master would designate. Readers of Herrick have tried for years to discover which, if any of them, had a counterpart in real life. Anthea, Electra, Sapho, Myrha, Corinna, Perilla, all are mentioned at least seven times, and Julia more than fifty. All the mistresses are identified with flowers, but Julia is pre-eminently the rose. She is the Queen-Priest who is to burn incense to appease love "for our very-many Trespasses." It is she who is asked to throw his book into the fire if the poet dies before it is completed. But, for all the attention she receives, is she, as Edmund Gosse seems to think, any more real than the others?

If she is, it seems strange that the most graphically

sensual of the poems, "The Vine," should concern not Julia but Lucia. And what of Corinna, one of the mistresses least frequently mentioned, but who receives the tribute of one of the most elaborate poems? Herrick is precise in his detail and everything in his book seems to be there for a reason. We, therefore, naturally expect that the names he gives his mistresses have some significance. And yet while he is precise, he is purposely vague in wishing to give an all-pervading dreamlike quality to his work. His mistresses drift in and out of his pages as delicate as the silk that clothes them and as insubstantial as the air that surrounds them. If there is any reason for the names, it is usually the verbal setting. In the poem "Being once blind, his request to Biancha," the name, meaning white, is appropriate for the contrast with darkness imagined in the poem; and the *b*'s prepare the reader for the falls and stumblings of the blind man mentioned. No other name could possibly be substituted in the famous line:

Come, my *Corinna*, come, let's goe a Maying.

It does not matter that Corinna was the feigned lady love of Ovid (and of many other poets); she here becomes the only Corinna who has ever existed, and the only one associated with Maytime and the country.

Miss Helen Bevington has called our attention recently in a most amusing way to the curious fact that Julia had a double chin.

Black and rowling is her eye,
Double chinn'd, and forehead high

writes Herrick. The detail is not so curious, however, if we think of Julia, as presented in the poems, as rather less than life-size. Herrick lays such stress on the daintiness and simplicity of his mistresses and on the smallness of their features that his reader begins to wonder if he is speaking of grown women at all. He is, of course, since there is nothing morbid in his portrayal, but the girls *are* girls rather than women, and like Ronsard's nymphets they have the plump and pleasing features of children.

Following these nymphs and shepherdesses through the pages of the *Hesperides*, the reader cannot escape the feeling that he is witnessing the enactment of a series of scenes by Roman *amorini*. The games of these maidens and these "younglings" are children's games—and Herrick made use of all the children's games of his day, push-pin, chop-cherry, cherry-pit, stoolball—but they naturally play all the adult games as well since they are projections of adult feeling. Herrick loved real children, and many of his poems are addressed to them. But his dream children are his greater love. They never existed, and they never will exist, except in a pagan paradise where experience is innocence and where sex is as natural as the air one breathes. They exist side by side with the fairies of Herrick's England. They belong to the western isles that he imagined, the Eden on earth, that is inevitably linked with childhood.

All this is not to say, of course, that Herrick did not know women intimately. He insists, quoting Ovid, that although his muse was jocund, his life was chaste, but he protests too much and one cannot believe that he expects to be taken literally. He was thirty-two years old before he entered the church, and certainly during his years in London he had ample opportunity for a worldly life. But even when he is writing of women that we know existed, he often makes us see them, if only briefly, in miniature. This is not in any sense a diminution of their value nor is it merely a reflection of the Anacreontic spirit of his day; it is his own peculiar angle of vision that carries over even into his longest and most serious pieces. Herrick's merry nature loved infinite variety. He treated language as if it were an accordion: his stanzas open from the shortest to the longest lines and close back again. His eye ranges over the broadest landscape only to come to rest on the most minute detail, and from there to return to the whole. In this same fashion, he can move from the world of the imagination to the world of everyday reality without the slightest difficulty. He can put scenes of pagan rites side by side with the rural customs of the Devonshire of his day, and he can reconcile Christianity with an eroticism that is virtually Oriental.

In the true spirit of the Renaissance, Herrick wanted to encompass everything, the old and the new, the good and the bad. For him it was all part of the great wheel of life, and the circle is one of his favorite figures. In Julia's petticoat he sees all the splendors of the heavens, and in a fly in amber, Cleopatra in her tomb. If the reader of the *Hesperides* finds himself pelted with roses and sprinkled with perfumes and spices on every page, he also encounters other sights and odors that have not been to everyone's liking. Herrick's epigrams have always been a source of embarrassment to his editors. (Pollard in his 1897 edition printed them, along with the other objectionable poems, in a detachable appendix.) "It is one of the paradoxes of literature," writes Percy Simpson in his introduction to his Oxford reprint of Herrick, "that this exquisite artist, experimenting in minute satire, should have composed a monotonous and, on the whole, pointless series of poems on merely nauseous themes. A reprint of Herrick among the Oxford Poets, side by side with the complete text already issued, gives a welcome opportunity of clearing away these weeds from the flower-garden of the *Hesperides*." Herrick's reaction to this would have been that every flower-garden, however formal, must have its weeds. The flowers shine all the brighter by reason of the contrast just as jewels are best seen against the dark. Perfection must have its flaw; a "sweet disorder" in a lady's dress is not only desirable but necessary since it heightens and accentuates the lady's beauty:

> Love's of it self, too sweet; the best of all
> Is, when loves hony has a dash of gall.

Herrick's is a bitter-sweet world, and to remove the bitter completely is to do injustice to the sweet since the two are inseparable.

Weeds, by their very nature, must be rank and lush; flowers are nourished by compost. If Herrick's flowers are children, symbols of love, his weeds are the aged, emblems of hate. It is true, as Marchette Chute remarks, that the individuality of Herrick's epigrams lies in "their real, ruthless hatred of physical ugliness." "He cannot hide his fury," she writes, "at the existence of bleary eyes and sweaty feet, toothless gums and bad breath. His delight in the surface of things—silks, flowers, perfumes, crystals, the softness of a woman's flesh—made him feel a sense of betrayal when they disappeared; and he turned on the pitiless victims of poverty and old age with the slingshot pebbles of his epigrams." When Herrick writes of silks, flowers, jewels, he describes their surface brilliance in order to stress the greater loveliness that lies beneath them or the deeper beauty that they exemplify. In his epigrams, however, he remains on the surface—with the traits of physical decay—and does not relate their foul aspect to life and death. This is their defect; they have no dimension.

The epigrams stand in the foreground of Herrick's landscape; they are surface blotches that hold the eye, even if only momentarily, rather than let it wander in perspective to ever-deepening vistas. The best of them do have, as Edmund Gosse remarks, a broad Pantagruelist humor, but in them Herrick is usually too close to his subject; the results are blurred and muddied. The finest of Herrick's poems are little dramas, sparkling with action; his epigrams are static. They present gross, larger-than-life, caricatures, drawn without relish.

In "Oberons Palace," after a long and highly intricate description of a miniature fairyland, the poem ends with these words: "This flax is spun," i.e., the web is completed, the matter has been dealt with. We may indeed look upon many of Herrick's poems as woven together since the texture appears to be the most important element: they are made up of shining surfaces, and are technically brilliant in the flash and interplay of the facets of words one upon another. Often the play is the point, and the surface is the subject. But is there nothing beneath that surface? "The important thing about a poet," A.E. said, "is finally this: 'Out of how deep a life does he speak?'" How deep, then, is Herrick?

II

Let us look at two six-line poems, each concerned with a surface that particularly interested Herrick, *i.e.*, silk. "The silken Snake" is the epitome of the diminutive Herrick:

> For sport my *Julia* threw a Lace
> Of silke and silver at my face:
> Watchet the silke was; and did make
> A shew, as if't'ad been a snake:
> The suddenness did me affright;
> But though it scar'd, it did not bite.

From the point of view of sound, the subject is immediately and perfectly conveyed. What other poet has used s's more tellingly, and turned that most defeating of consonants into such a small triumph? The subtle alternation of s and *l* throughout presents the slithering of the snake: at once the snaky quality of the silk becomes the silken quality of the snake; and the alternating short and long vowels suggest the snake's uncoiling and striking. The long *a*'s, coming at the end of each of the first four lines, carry forward the feeling of the coldness of the silk, that reaches its climax in the word "snake" and its dénouement in the word "scar'd." "Watchet" is, of course, a cold blue-green, sky-blue, a serpent's flashing blue, cold to the eye. The poet plays throughout with dental sounds, suggesting with them the play of the serpent's tongue: we have them in the very word for the silk's color "watchet," and then the final flickering in the fourth line "as if't'ad been a snake." The dentals, tripping up the tongue, draw attention away from the other consonants and from the uncoiling effect of the vowels, and rightly so because they are concerned with presenting the poem's most important element—the serpent's bite. The fact that the serpent has no bite is the poem's point, and its conclusion.

In Herrick's Eden the serpent is a child's toy, and its purpose is play. The snake, rather than destroying its victim, startles him and awakens him with its coldness. But the snake is the silk and the silver, and in the phrase

"Watchet the silke was" there is in the sound of the *w*'s and the *a*'s an effect completely opposed to that of coldness. While the color gives coldness to the eye, the words themselves convey warmth to the ear. We realize that irony has been minutely at work, for the total effect on the reader is not one of chill, but of amusement and warmth.

Herrick's careful understatement builds by indirection, and the simile of the snake takes the reader away from the over-all metaphor. This is a "silken" snake, but the most important word in the poem is "Lace." The simile of the snake is loose and ambiguous; it is a lace of silk and silver that Julia throws. The lace is, of course, Julia's girdle, made of an open-work fabric of silk and silver threads, inwrought probably with patterns. The lace becomes the snake, but being lace, it remains the surface, the cold skin, of the snake. Its loops, uncoiling, present the snake striking, but the lace is still a net. The poet, rather than being bitten by the serpent, is enmeshed in its scales: the surface literally triumphs.

In another, and far greater, lyric concerned with silk, "Upon Julia's Clothes," the sounds again constitute one of the triumphs of English poetry:

> When as in silks my *Julia* goes,
> Then, then (me thinks) how sweetly flowes
> That liquefaction of her clothes.
>
> Next, when I cast mine eyes and see
> That brave Vibration each way free;
> O how that glittering taketh me!

We have again in the first three lines the mellifluent quality of silk in the *s*'s and *l*'s, and again in the over-all vowel pattern of the poem; and in the alternation of long and short vowel sounds, first, the flow of silk and then, its frou-frou and crinkle. Dr. Tillyard says: "A fresh and unaffected sensuality pervades the poem. Not only is the speaker's excitement expressed by 'then, then,' but from the flow of the clothes and their vibration the hint of the body beneath is not absent. The full emphasis and the fall of the third line express how well the spectator's excitement is satisfied by the downward flow of the silk. We may even derive from 'liquefaction' a hint of the word 'satisfaction.' 'Liquefaction' is a sophisticated word, and as such is more important than as describing a quality of silk which (incidentally) had been already indicated in the word 'flows.' More important probably than any of the factors noted above is the contrast on which the poem is constructed. The spectator first sees the downward flow of Julia's silks and he experiences satisfaction. He then sees the silks vibrating, perhaps moving in little horizontal eddies, and he is captivated. . . ." Dr. Tillyard, in his concern with the oblique, has been a victim of Herrick's obliquity. There is, of course, far more than a "hint of the body" beneath the clothes. What Herrick is saying of Julia is quite simply: (a) I like her with her clothes on, and (b) I far prefer her with them off. But Dr. Tillyard is not alone in being misled in this case. Herrick's mastery of sound, as evidenced in the first three lines, has made many readers believe this to be, as it indeed is, one of the finest poems on silk ever written. But it is much more than that.

For a poem whose chief appeal is sensuous, the language is strangely abstract. The two most important words in these six lines are "liquefaction" and "vibration," both abstract—and sophisticated, as Dr. Tillyard observes—nouns of Latin derivation, "liquefaction" meaning the act or process of making or becoming liquid, or the state of being a liquid. And here, of course, it is both things: the silk becomes water, and is water. "Vibration" means oscillation; and suggests immediately the moving to and fro of the silk and of the lady's body, that is, the liquid not only moves, flows, it also oscillates and glitters. There is a progression in the poem underlined by the words, "Then, then," and the word "Next," that opens the second stanza. The lines do not merely say that Julia's silks are like water, and that when she walks, they move glittering back and forth. The words "each way free" can only mean unconfined in every direction. The silk surely cannot be said to be entirely free; what is free must be Julia's body. The lady's clothes have been removed, or are being removed, before our eyes, and what Herrick is saying, as he does so often, is that he prefers the nude to the clothed figure, no matter how lovely the fabric that covers it, that he prefers nature to art. The central metaphor of the first tercet is that of a river flowing forward, confined within its banks; that of the second, the waves of an ocean moving freely to and fro, and all is contained within the abstract framework of "liquefaction" and "vibration." In the first tercet, it is the external qualities of the lady, her dress, that impress themselves on the internal in the observer, the mind, "me thinks." In the second, the situation is reversed; it is the internal, the lady's body that impresses itself on the external, the eyes, the vision of the beholder.

We have witnessed in the poem a peculiar alchemical process whereby a base material is transformed before our eyes into gold; and it is no mere accident that the entire work hinges on a word with alchemical overtones, for the alchemist, like the poet, while going through his complicated labors, may be said, in a sense, to have explored the depths of the human unconscious. Herrick, in his early years an apprenticed goldsmith, has wrought with the mind a metal of inestimable value. And it is not too far-fetched to say that his work as a goldsmith in some ways prepared him for the greater and more difficult craft of poetry.

Many of Herrick's poems treat the same subject. In "Clothes do but cheat and cousen us," he writes, "mine Eye / Is wone with flesh, not *Drapery*," just as his master Ben Jonson had said: "Such sweet neglect more taketh me / Than all the adulteries of art." "To his Mistresses" of Herrick also provides a parallel:

Put on your silks; and piece by piece
Give them the scent of Amber-Greece:
And for your breaths too, let them smell
Ambrosia-like, or *Nectarell*:
While other Gums their sweets perspire,
By your owne jewels set on fire.

So likewise, in this poem, it is the lady's "owne jewels" which fire the silk.

Now if this poems fails in any respect, the reason must lie in the fact that the surface is so skillfully presented that it attracts undue attention to itself at the expense of the basic content. Here is a work of art of which it may be said that the texture is the text: it is concerned with the texture of woman's clothing, but more than that, with the texture of her flesh. If it is often taken to be merely a description of the quality of silk, it must be because the mellifluence of silk is so powerfully expressed in the word "liquefaction" that the reader is almost forced to view the second stanza as a mere amplification and restatement of the first. But the reader is at fault then in not appreciating the full subtlety of the poem, and in missing the impact of Herrick's miniature drama.

Several critics have been aware of "the hint of the body" in this poem, but a good deal of nonsense has been written about Julia's extraordinary physical features accentuated by the glittering of overlaid silk. In *The Personal Heresy: A Controversy,* Dr. Tillyard and Mr. C. S. Lewis argue for pages on the subject. Mr. Lewis holds that what the poem tells him about is silk; the experience the poet is communicating is one the poet had regarding silk. Dr. Tillyard contends that Mr. Lewis is concerned only with things, and that it is the state of the poet's mind that is communicated, "the qualities of unaffected sensuality, keen observation, sophistication, and sense of decorum." While the critics keep bickering, not unlike two women over a bolt of silk at a counter, Julia in all her unadorned splendor has passed them by. And Herrick continues to smile from between the lines.

Both the poems we have been discussing might have been written by a painter; they are clearly the work of a poet for whom the visual imagination is paramount. In each case, it is the eyes that act and are acted upon. The exciting "glittering" of Julia's nudity "taketh" the whole poet, but it reaches him through his eyes; the excitement is visual. In the case of the silken snake, there is the same type of "glittering" connection between the poet and his mistress. In that poem, however, it is the mistress rather than the poet who casts the glance, and it is a captivating one. The girdle of blue silk and silver is also a metaphor for Julia's tempting and flirtatious gaze, her rolling eye. Both pieces present us with miniature dramas enacted in the boudoir. Both are concerned with surfaces, with the clothed and the unclothed figure; and both are indeed the works of an "unaffected sensuality." What is most important, as so frequently in Herrick, is, of course, what is left out. There is clearly a before and after, and therefore the poems expand in their small frames. We need not dwell at length on the sexual implications of "The silken Snake." A psychologist might devote pages to a study of the male and female symbolism in these six lines. This is a trifle, and Herrick is here playing with play; it is all "for sport." But even in this lesser lyric the vision of depth should not be lost because of the surface shimmer. A greater lyric like "Upon Julia's Clothes" has retained our attention because it is at the same time so simple and direct and so endlessly complex.

In his sonnet "Pur Sang" on one of his favorite pictorial subjects, a racehorse, Edgar Degas speaks of the horse as:

Tout nerveusement nu dans sa robe de soie.

Herrick's Julia is likewise "nervously naked in her silken gown." And the diminutive ballerinas of Degas come to mind in connection with Herrick, for Degas also created a world of his own, based on the real world but apart from it, in which delicate and lovely figures move, animated by feeling. Herrick was a lover of beautiful things and not of human beings in the ordinary sense. If we want people presented as in Chaucer, we shall not find them here; Herrick's beings are projections, distillations, of human feeling; and for those readers for whom "feeling is first" he will have no inferior. It has been said that there is something inhuman about the ballet as an art form: it may appear devoid of feeling because it is *all* feeling. Although Herrick may seem at first merely childlike, playful, and innocent, it is the maturity of his feeling that in the end must command our attention. And, in this sense, he is surely not without depth, for feeling may have a complexity of quite a different order from that of thought. Viewed from this angle, Herrick is as mature as Donne, although to modern, if not to Elizabethan, eyes he may appear as far removed as it is possible to be.

In pointing out some of the rewards of reading Herrick, I have only touched the surface, but I have tried to show how intricate and deceptive that surface can be. "With an old serving-woman in a tumbledown country parsonage," Edmund Gosse said of Herrick, "his life passed merrily among such dreams as Oriental sultans wear themselves out to realize." And yet for all the brightness of his dreams, he has his darker side that cannot escape the careful reader. Grosart found that the "unlifted shadow of melancholy must have lain broad and black over Herrick." His merry nature had a "dark thread interwoven in it." Herrick may not appear to insist upon it, but then it is not his nature to insist. He prefers a music that "sighs" rather than "sounds." But for all his instinctive gaiety, he could write:

> Putrefaction is the end
> Of all that Nature doth entend.

And death is a theme recurring on every page. Professor Musgrove has pointed out that Herrick's series of poems on women's clothes is not complete without the silks as seen "with more serious eye, as the vesture of decay," as in "The Transfiguration":

> Immortall clothing I put on,
> So soone as *Julia* I am gon
> To mine eternall Mansion.

> Thou, thou art here, to humane sight
> Cloth'd all with incorrupted light;
> But yet how more admir'dly bright

> Wilt thou appear, when thou art set
> In thy refulgent Thronelet,
> That shin'st thus in thy counterfeit?

Herrick leaves much to his reader; the very nature of his art is to conceal itself. But a vision such as this, at once so contained and so transcendent, will always hold the attention of those for whom the imagination has value.

WILLIAM JAY SMITH
October 1961

BIBLIOGRAPHY

Works:

The Poetical Works of Robert Herrick, edited by L. C. Martin. (Oxford, 1956.)
(The text of this volume, which follows that of the original edition of *Hesperides,* published in 1648, has been used in this selection.)

The Complete Poems of Robert Herrick, edited with memorial-introduction and notes by the Rev. Alexander B. Grosart, 3 vols. (London, 1876.)

Robert Herrick, the Hesperides & Noble Numbers, edited by Alfred Pollard with a preface by A. C. Swinburne, 2 vols., the "Muses' Library." (London and New York, 1898.)

A Concordance to the Poems of Robert Herrick, compiled and edited by Malcolm MacLeod. (New York, 1936.)

Selected Poems:

The Poetical Works of Robert Herrick, edited by F. W. Moorman with a prefatory note by Percy Simpson. (London, 1947.)

Chrysomela, a Selection from the Lyrical Poems of Robert Herrick, arranged with notes by Francis Turner Palgrave. (London and New York, 1888.)

The Poems of Robert Herrick, edited with a biographical introduction by John Masefield, "The Chapbooks." (London, 1906.)

Seventeenth-Century Lyrics, edited with short biographies, bibliographies, and notes by Alexander Corbin Judson. (Chicago, 1927.)

Biographical and Critical Studies:

Robert Herrick: A Biographical and Critical Study, by F. W. Moorman. (London, 1910.)

Robert Herrick: Contribution à l'Etude de la Poésie Lyrique en Angleterre au Dix-septième Siècle, by Floris Delattre. (Paris, 1912.)

Two Gentle Men, the Lives of George Herbert and Robert Herrick, by Marchette Chute. (New York, 1959.)

Seventeenth Century Studies, by Edmund Gosse. (London, 1883.)

The Universe of Robert Herrick, by S. Musgrove, Auckland University College English series no. 4. (Auckland, 1950.)

Classical Influence on the Tribe of Ben, by Kathryn Anderson McEuen. (Cedar Rapids, 1939.)

The Well Wrought Urn, Studies in the Structure of Poetry, by Cleanth Brooks. (New York, 1947.)

Bibliography:

Robert Herrick (A Concise Bibliography), by Samuel A. Tannenbaum and Dorothy R. Tannenbaum, Elizabethan Bibliographies, no. 40. (New York, 1949.)

Chronology

1591 Born August 24, of a prominent family of Leicester, the son of Nicholas Herrick (Eyrick), who had migrated to London and established himself as goldsmith and banker, and Julian Stone Herrick, the last of seven children.

1592 Father, Nicholas, died falling from a window of house in Goldsmiths' Row, having apparently committed suicide; two days earlier he had made out a will describing himself as "sick in body."

1607 On September 25, at age of sixteen, apprenticed to his uncle, Sir William Herrick, a goldsmith in London.

1613 Entered St. John's College, Cambridge, as a fellow-commoner. Letters to his uncle at this time all contained requests for money.

1617 Transferred to Trinity Hall, Cambridge, to save money and to study law. Graduated with a B.A.

1620 Took degree of M.A.

1623 Ordained as deacon in the Church of England on April 24, and priest on April 25.
At some time during this period came under the influence of Ben Jonson, then the most influential writer in England; was one of the "Tribe of Ben."

1625 Was well known as a poet, as is shown by reference to him in *The Muses' Dirge*, written on the death of King James. (This was one of the few compliments paid him during his lifetime.)

1627 Went on expedition to the Isle of Rhé as chaplain to its leader, the Duke of Buckingham; two-thirds of the men sent out did not return.

1630 After failure of expedition and assassination of Buckingham, Herrick made vicar of Dean Prior in Devonshire.

1640 Was in London at this time, and made attempts to have his book published. A report by William Dell, secretary to the Archbishop of Canterbury, asserts that he had been living in Westminster and was father of an illegitimate child by Thomasin Parsons.

1647 Ejected from Dean Prior, retired to London, where he subsisted on charity until the Restoration.

1648 Publication of *Hesperides*, containing also *His Noble Numbers*; the book found no market.

1650 Seventy-five of Herrick's poems printed without credit in the anthology, *Wit's Recreations*.

1674 Buried on October 15 at Dean Prior.

The Argument of his Book

I sing of *Brooks*, of *Blossomes*, *Birds*, and *Bowers*:*
Of *April*, *May*, of *June*, and *July*-Flowers.
I sing of *May-poles*, *Hock-carts*, *Wassails*, *Wakes*,
Of *Bride-grooms*, *Brides*, and of their *Bridall-cakes*.
I write of *Youth*, of *Love*, and have Accesse
By these, to sing of cleanly-*Wantonnesse*.
I sing of *Dewes*, of *Raines*, and piece by piece
Of *Balme*, of *Oyle*, of *Spice*, and *Amber-Greece*.
I sing of *Times trans-shifting*; and I write
How *Roses* first came *Red*, and *Lillies White*,   10
I write of *Groves*, of *Twilights*, and I sing
The Court of *Mab*, and of the *Fairie-King*.
I write of *Hell*: I sing (and ever shall)
Of *Heaven*, and hope to have it after all.

When he would have his verses read

In sober mornings, doe not thou reherse
The holy incantation of a verse;
But when that men have both well drunke, and fed,
Let my Enchantments then be sung, or read.
When Laurell spirts 'ith fire, and when the Hearth
Smiles to it selfe, and guilds the roofe with mirth;
When up the *Thyrse*** is rais'd, and when the sound
Of sacred *Orgies*** flyes, A round, A round.
When the *Rose* raignes, and locks with ointments shine,
Let rigid *Cato* read these Lines of mine.   10

* The editor's notes appear together beginning on page
152. Herrick's own notes appear at the foot of the page
of text where they occur.

  **A *Javeline* twind with *Ivy*.
 ***Songs to *Bacchus*.

The Parliament of Roses to Julia

I dreamt the Roses one time went
To meet and sit in Parliament:
The place for these, and for the rest
Of flowers, was thy spotlesse breast:
Over the which a State was drawne
Of Tiffanie, or Cob-web Lawne;
Then in that *Parly,* all those powers
Voted the Rose; the Queen of flowers.
But so, as that her self should be
The maide of Honour unto thee.   10

To his Mistresses

Helpe me! helpe me! now I call
To my pretty *Witchcrafts* all:
Old I am, and cannot do
That, I was accustom'd to.
Bring your *Magicks, Spels, and Charmes,*
To enflesh my thighs, and armes:
Is there no way to beget
In my limbs their former heat?
Æson had (as *Poets* faine)
Baths that made him young againe: 10
Find that *Medicine* (if you can)
For your drie-decrepid man:
Who would faine his strength renew,
Were it but to pleasure you.

Soft Musick

The mellow touch of musick most doth wound
The soule, when it doth rather sigh, then sound.

The shooe tying

Anthea bade me tye her shooe;
I did; and kist the Instep too:
And would have kist unto her knee,
Had not her Blush rebuked me.

Why Flowers change colour

These fresh beauties (we can prove)
Once were Virgins sick of love,
Turn'd to Flowers. Still in some
Colours goe, and colours come.

The Vine

I dream'd this mortal part of mine
Was Metamorphoz'd to a Vine;
Which crawling one and every way,
Enthrall'd my dainty *Lucia.*
Me thought, her long small legs & thighs
I with my *Tendrils* did surprize;
Her Belly, Buttocks, and her Waste
By my soft *Nerv'lits* were embrac'd:
About her head I writhing hung,
And with rich clusters (hid among
The leaves) her temples I behung:
So that my *Lucia* seem'd to me
Young *Bacchus* ravisht by his tree.
My curles about her neck did craule,
And armes and hands they did enthrall:
So that she could not freely stir,
(All parts there made one prisoner.)
But when I crept with leaves to hide

10

Those parts, which maids keep unespy'd,
Such fleeting pleasures there I took,
That with the fancie I awook;
And found (Ah me!) this flesh of mine
More like a *Stock,* then like a *Vine.*

Love's play at Push-pin

Love and my selfe (beleeve me) on a day
At childish Push-pin (for our sport) did play:
I put, he pusht, and heedless of my skin,
Love prickt my finger with a golden pin:
Since which, it festers so, that I can prove
'Twas but a trick to poyson me with love:
Little the wound was; greater was the smart;
The finger bled, but burnt was all my heart.

Cherrie-ripe

Cherrie-Ripe, Ripe, Ripe, I cry,
Full and faire ones; come and buy:
If so be, you ask me where
They doe grow? I answer, There,
Where my *Julia's* lips doe smile;
There's the Land, or Cherry-Ile:
Whose Plantations fully show
All the yeere, where Cherries grow.

To his Mistresses

Put on your silks; and piece by piece
Give them the scent of Amber-Greece:
And for your breaths too, let them smell
Ambrosia-like, or *Nectarell:*

[To his Mistresses]　34

While other Gums their sweets perspire,
By your owne jewels set on fire.

His request to Julia

Julia, if I chance to die
Ere I print my Poetry;
I most humbly thee desire
To commit it to the fire:
Better 'twere my Book were dead,
Then to live not perfected.

All things decay and die

All things decay with Time: The Forrest sees
The growth, and down-fall of her aged trees:
That Timber tall, which three-score *lusters* stood
The proud *Dictator* of the State-like wood:
I meane (the Soveraigne of all Plants) the Oke
Droops, dies, and falls without the cleavers stroke.

TO THE KING, Upon his comming with his Army into the West

Welcome, most welcome to our Vowes and us,
Most great, and universall *Genius!*
The Drooping West, which hitherto has stood
As one, in long-lamented-widow-hood;
Looks like a Bride now, or a bed of flowers,
Newly refresh't, both by the Sun, and showers.
War, which before was horrid, now appears
Lovely in you, brave Prince of Cavaliers!
A deale of courage in each bosome springs
By your accesse; (*O you the best of Kings!*)   10

Ride on with all white *Omens;* so, that where
Your Standard's up, we fix a Conquest there.

To the reverend shade of his religious Father

That for seven *Lusters* I did never come
To doe the *Rites* to thy Religious Tombe:
That neither haire was cut, or true teares shed
By me, o'r thee, *(as justments to the dead)*
Forgive, forgive me; since I did not know
Whether thy bones had here their Rest, or no.
But now 'tis known, Behold; behold, I bring
Unto thy Ghost, th'Effused Offering:
And look, what Smallage, Night-shade, Cypresse, Yew,
Unto the shades have been, or now are due,   10
Here I devote; And something more then so;
I come to pay a Debt of Birth I owe.
Thou gav'st me life, (but Mortall;) For that one
Favour, Ile make full satisfaction;
For my life mortall, Rise from out thy Herse,
And take a life immortall from my Verse.

Delight in Disorder

A sweet disorder in the dresse
Kindles in cloathes a wantonnesse:
A Lawne about the shoulders thrown
Into a fine distraction:
An erring Lace, which here and there
Enthralls the Crimson Stomacher:
A Cuffe neglectfull, and thereby
Ribbands to flow confusedly:
A winning wave (deserving Note)
In the tempestuous petticote: 10
A carelesse shooe-string, in whose tye
I see a wilde civility:
Doe more bewitch me, then when Art
Is too precise in every part.

To Dean-bourn, a rude River in Devon, by which sometimes he lived

Dean-bourn, farewell: I never look to see
Deane, or thy warty incivility.
Thy rockie bottome, that doth teare thy streams,
And makes them frantick, ev'n to all extreames;
To my content, I never sho'd behold,
Were thy streames silver, or thy rocks all gold.
Rockie thou art; and rockie we discover
Thy men; and rockie are thy wayes all over.
O men, O manners: Now, and ever knowne
To be *A Rockie Generation!*   10
A people currish; churlish as the seas;
And rude (almost) as rudest Salvages.
With whom I did, and may re-sojourne when
Rockes turn to Rivers, Rivers turn to Men.

His Cavalier

Give me that man, that dares bestride
The active Sea-horse, & with pride,
Through that huge field of waters ride:
Who, with his looks too, can appease
The ruffling winds and raging Seas,
In mid'st of all their outrages.
This, this a virtuous man can doe,
Saile against Rocks, and split them too;
I! and a world of Pikes passe through.

To Criticks

Ile write, because Ile give
You Criticks means to live:
For sho'd I not supply
The Cause, th'effect wo'd die.

Upon Blanch

Blanch swears her Husband's lovely; when a scald
Has blear'd his eyes: Besides, his head is bald
Next, his wilde eares, like Lethern wings full spread,
Flutter to flie, and beare away his head.

Barly-Break: or, Last in Hell

We two are last in Hell: what may we feare
To be tormented, or kept Pris'ners here?
Alas! If kissing be of plagues the worst,
We'll wish, in Hell we had been Last and First.

A Country life

TO HIS BROTHER, M. THO: HERRICK

Thrice, and above, blest (my soules halfe) art thou,
  In thy both Last, and Better Vow:
Could'st leave the City, for exchange, to see
  The Countries sweet simplicity:
And it to know, and practice; with intent
  To grow the sooner innocent:
By studying to know vertue; and to aime
  More at her nature, then her name:
The last is but the least; the first doth tell
  Wayes lesse to live, then to live well: 10
And both are knowne to thee, who now can'st live
  Led by thy conscience; to give
Justice to soone-pleas'd nature; and to show,
  Wisdome and she together goe,
And keep one Centre: This with that conspires,
  To teach Man to confine desires:
And know, that Riches have their proper stint,
  In the contented mind, not mint.
And can'st instruct, that those who have the itch
  Of craving more, are never rich.   20
These things thou know'st to'th'height, and dost prevent

That plague; because thou art content
With that Heav'n gave thee with a warie hand,
(More blessed in thy Brasse, then Land)
To keep cheap Nature even, and upright;
To coole, not cocker Appetite.
Thus thou canst tearcely live to satisfie
The belly chiefly; not the eye:
Keeping the barking stomach wisely quiet,
Lesse with a neat, then needfull diet. 30
But that which most makes sweet thy country life,
Is, the fruition of a wife:
Whom (Stars consenting with thy Fate) thou hast
Got, not so beautifull, as chast:
By whose warme side thou dost securely sleep
(While Love the Centinell doth keep)
With those deeds done by day, which n'er affright
Thy silken slumbers in the night.
Nor has the darknesse power to usher in
Feare to those sheets, that know no sin. 40
But still thy wife, by chast intentions led,
Gives thee each night a Maidenhead.
The Damaskt medowes, and the peebly streames
Sweeten, and make soft your dreames:
The Purling springs, groves, birds, and well-weav'd Bowrs,
With fields enameled with flowers,
Present their shapes; while fantasie discloses
Millions of *Lillies* mixt with *Roses*.
Then dream, ye heare the Lamb by many a bleat
Woo'd to come suck the milkie Teat: 50
While *Faunus* in the Vision comes to keep,
From rav'ning wolves, the fleecie sheep.
With thousand such enchanting dreams, that meet
To make sleep not so sound, as sweet:
Nor can these figures so thy rest endeare,
As not to rise when *Chanticlere*
Warnes the last Watch; but with the Dawne dost rise
To work, but first to sacrifice;
Making thy peace with heav'n, for some late fault,
With Holy-meale, and spirting-salt. 60
Which done, thy painfull Thumb this sentence tells us,

Love for our labour all things sells us.
Nor are thy daily and devout affaires
    Attended with those desp'rate cares,
Th'industrious Merchant has; who for to find
    Gold, runneth to the Western Inde,
And back again, (tortur'd with fears) doth fly,
    Untaught, to suffer Poverty.
But thou at home, blest with securest ease,
    Sitt'st, and beleev'st that there be seas,   70
And watrie dangers; while thy whiter hap,
    But seest these things within thy Map.
And viewing them with a more safe survey,
    Mak'st easie Feare unto thee say,
A heart thrice wall'd with Oke, and Brasse, that man
    Had, first, durst plow the Ocean.
But thou at home without or tyde or gale,
    Canst in thy Map securely saile:
Seeing those painted Countries; and so guesse
    By those fine Shades, their Substances: 80
And from thy Compasse taking small advice,
    Buy'st Travell at the lowest price.
Nor are thine eares so deafe, but thou canst heare
    (Far more with wonder, then with feare)
Fame tell of States, of Countries, Courts, and Kings;
    And beleeve there be such things:
When of these truths, thy happyer knowledge lyes,
    More in thine eares, then in thine eyes.
And when thou hear'st by that too-true-Report,
    Vice rules the Most, or All at Court: 90
Thy pious wishes are, (though thou not there)
    Vertue had, and mov'd her Sphere.
But thou liv'st fearlesse; and thy face ne'r shewes
    Fortune when she comes, or goes.
But with thy equall thoughts, prepar'd dost stand,
    To take her by the either hand:
Nor car'st which comes the first, the foule or faire;
    A wise man ev'ry way lies square.
And like a surly *Oke* with storms perplext;
    Growes still the stronger, strongly vext.   100
Be so, bold spirit; Stand Center-like, unmov'd;

And be not onely thought, but prov'd
To be what I report thee; and inure
   Thy selfe, if want comes to endure:
And so thou dost: for thy desires are
   Confin'd to live with private *Larr:*
Not curious whether Appetite be fed,
   Or with the first, or second bread.
Who keep'st no proud mouth for delicious cates:
   Hunger makes coorse meats, delicates.   110
Can'st, and unurg'd, forsake that Larded fare,
   Which Art, not Nature, makes so rare;
To taste boyl'd Nettles, Colworts, Beets, and eate
   These, and sowre herbs, as dainty meat?
While soft Opinion makes thy *Genius* say,
   Content makes all Ambrosia.
Nor is it, that thou keep'st this stricter size
   So much for want, as exercise:
To numb the sence of Dearth, which sho'd sinne haste it,
   Thou might'st but onely see't, not taste it.   120
Yet can thy humble roofe maintaine a Quire
   Of singing Crickits by thy fire:
And the brisk Mouse may feast her selfe with crums,
   Till that the green-ey'd Kitling comes.
Then to her Cabbin, blest she can escape
   The sudden danger of a Rape.
And thus thy little-well-kept-stock doth prove,
   Wealth cannot make a life, but Love.
Nor art thou so close-handed, but can'st spend
   (Counsell concurring with the end)   130
As well as spare: still conning o'r this Theame,
   To shun the first, and last extreame.
Ordaining that thy small stock find no breach,
   Or to exceed thy Tether's reach:
But to live round, and close, and wisely true
   To thine owne selfe; and knowne to few.
Thus let thy Rurall Sanctuary be
   Elizium to thy wife and thee;
There to disport your selves with golden measure:
   For seldome use commends the pleasure.   140
Live, and live blest; thrice happy Paire; Let Breath,

But lost to one, be th'others death.
And as there is one Love, one Faith, one Troth,
  Be so one Death, one Grave to both.
Till when, in such assurance live, ye may
  Nor feare, or wish your dying day.

To the Painter, to draw him a Picture

Come, skilfull *Lupo*, now, and take
Thy *Bice*, thy *Umber*, *Pink*, and *Lake*;
And let it be thy Pensils strife,
To paint a Bridgeman to the life:
Draw him as like too, as you can,
An old, poore, lying, flatt'ring man:
His cheeks be-pimpled, red and blue;
His nose and lips of mulbrie hiew.
Then for an easie fansie; place
A Burling iron for his face: 10
Next, make his cheeks with breath to swell,
And for to speak, if possible:
But do not so; for feare, lest he
Sho'd by his breathing, poyson thee.

Upon Cuffe. Epig.

Cuffe comes to Church much; but he keeps his bed
Those Sundayes onely, when as Briefs are read.
This makes *Cuffe* dull; and troubles him the most,
Because he cannot sleep i'th'Church, free-cost.

The frozen Zone: or, Julia disdainfull

  Whither? Say, whither shall I fly,
  To slack these flames wherein I frie?
  To the Treasures, shall I goe,
  Of the Raine, Frost, Haile, and Snow?
  Shall I search the under-ground,

Where all Damps, and Mists are found?
Shall I seek (for speedy ease)
All the floods, and frozen seas?
Or descend into the deep,
Where eternall cold does keep? 10
These may coole; but there's a Zone
Colder yet then any one:
That's my *Julia's* breast; where dwels
Such destructive Ysicles;
As that the Congelation will
Me sooner starve, then those can kill.

An Epitaph upon a child

Virgins promis'd when I dy'd,
That they wo'd each Primrose-tide,
Duely, Morne and Ev'ning, come,
And with flowers dresse my Tomb.
Having promis'd, pay your debts,
Maids, and here strew Violets.

Upon Scobble. Epig.

Scobble for Whoredom whips his wife; and cryes,
He'll slit her nose; But blubb'ring, she replyes,
Good Sir, make no more cuts i'th'outward skin,
One slit's enough to let Adultry in.

His fare-well to Sack

Farewell thou Thing, time-past so knowne, so deare
To me, as blood to life and spirit: neare,
Nay, thou more neare then kindred, friend, man, wife,
Male to the female, soule to body: Life
To quick action, or the warme soft side
Of the resigning, yet resisting Bride.
The kisse of Virgins; First-fruits of the bed;

Soft speech, smooth touch, the lips, the Maiden-head:
These, and a thousand sweets, co'd never be
So neare, or deare, as thou wast once to me.　　　　10
O thou the drink of Gods, and Angels! Wine
That scatter'st Spirit and Lust; whose purest shine,
More radiant then the Summers Sun-beams shows;
Each way illustrious, brave; and like to those
Comets we see by night; whose shagg'd portents
Fore-tell the comming of some dire events:
Or some full flame, which with a pride aspires,
Throwing about his wild, and active fires.
'Tis thou, above Nectar, O Divinest soule!
(Eternall in thy self) that canst controule　　　　20
That, which subverts whole nature, grief and care;
Vexation of the mind, and damn'd Despaire.
'Tis thou, alone, who with thy Mistick Fan,
Work'st more then Wisdome, Art, or Nature can,
To rouze the sacred madnesse; and awake
The frost-bound-blood, and spirits; and to make
Them frantick with thy raptures, flashing through
The soule, like lightning, and as active too.
'Tis not *Apollo* can, or those thrice three
Castalian Sisters, sing, if wanting thee.　　　　30
Horace, Anacreon both had lost their fame,
Had'st thou not fill'd them with thy fire and flame.
Phæbean splendour! and thou *Thespian* spring!
Of which, sweet Swans must drink, before they sing
Their true-pac'd-Numbers, and their Holy-Layes,
Which makes them worthy *Cedar,* and the *Bayes.*
But why? why longer doe I gaze upon
Thee with the eye of admiration?
Since I must leave thee; and enforc'd, must say
To all thy witching beauties, Goe, Away.　　　　40
But if thy whimpring looks doe ask me why?
Then know, that Nature bids thee goe, not I.
'Tis her erroneous self has made a braine
Uncapable of such a Soveraigne,
As is thy powerfull selfe. Prethee not smile;
Or smile more inly; lest thy looks beguile
My vowes denounc'd in zeale, which thus much show thee,

[*His fare-well to Sack*]　　44

That I have sworn, but by thy looks to know thee.
Let others drink thee freely; and desire
Thee and their lips espous'd; while I admire,   50
And love thee; but not taste thee. Let my Muse
Faile of thy former helps; and onely use
Her inadult'rate strength: what's done by me
Hereafter, shall smell of the Lamp, not thee.

The Custard

For second course, last night, a Custard came
To th'board, so hot, as none co'd touch the same:
Furze, three or foure times with his cheeks did blow
Upon the Custard, and thus cooled so:
It seem'd by this time to admit the touch;
But none co'd eate it, 'cause it stunk so much.

The suspition upon his over-much familiarity with a Gentlewoman

And must we part, because some say,
Loud is our love, and loose our play,
And more then well becomes the day?
Alas for pitty! and for us
Most innocent, and injur'd thus.
Had we kept close, or play'd within,
Suspition now had been the sinne,
And shame had follow'd long ere this,
T'ave plagu'd, what now unpunisht is.
But we as fearlesse of the Sunne,   10
As faultlesse; will not wish undone,
What now is done: since *where no sin*
Unbolts the doore, no shame comes in.
Then comely and most fragrant Maid,
Be you more warie, then afraid
Of these Reports; because you see
The fairest most suspected be.
The common formes have no one eye,

Or eare of burning jealousie
To follow them: but chiefly, where   20
Love makes the cheek, and chin a sphere
To dance and play in: (Trust me) there
Suspicion questions every haire.
Come, you are faire; and sho'd be seen
While you are in your sprightfull green:
And what though you had been embrac't
By me, were you for that unchast?
No, no, no more then is yond' Moone,
Which shining in her perfect Noone;
In all that great and glorious light,   30
Continues cold, as is the night.
Then, beauteous Maid, you may retire;
And as for me, my chast desire
Shall move t'wards you; although I see
Your face no more: So live you free
From Fames black lips, as you from me.

Single life most secure

Suspicion, Discontent, and Strife,
Come in for Dowrie with a Wife.

Some comfort in calamity

To conquer'd men, some comfort 'tis to fall
By th'hand of him who is the Generall.

The Vision

Sitting alone (as one forsook)
Close by a Silver-shedding Brook;
With hands held up to Love, I wept;
And after sorrowes spent, I slept:
Then in a Vision I did see
A glorious forme appeare to me:

[The Vision]   46

A Virgins face she had; her dresse
Was like a sprightly *Spartanesse*.
A silver bow with green silk strung,
Down from her comely shoulders hung: 10
And as she stood, the wanton Aire
Dandled the ringlets of her haire.
Her legs were such *Diana* shows,
When tuckt up she a hunting goes;
With Buskins shortned to descrie
The happy dawning of her thigh:
Which when I saw, I made accesse
To kisse that tempting nakednesse:
But she forbad me, with a wand
Of Mirtle she had in her hand: 20
And chiding me, said, Hence, Remove,
Herrick, thou art too coorse to love.

Love me little, love me long

You say, to me-wards your affection's strong;
Pray love me little, so you love me long.
Slowly goes farre: The meane is best: Desire
Grown violent, do's either die, or tire.

Upon Strut

Strut, once a Fore-man of a Shop we knew;
But turn'd a Ladies Usher now, ('tis true:)
Tell me, has *Strut* got ere a title more?
No; he's but Fore-man, as he was before.

TO THE KING, To cure the Evill

To find that Tree of Life, whose Fruits did feed,
And Leaves did heale, all sick of humane seed:
To finde *Bethesda,* and an Angel there,
Stirring the waters, I am come; and here,

At last, I find, (after my much to doe)
The Tree, Bethesda, and the Angel too:
And all in Your Blest Hand, which has the powers
Of all those suppling-healing herbs and flowers.
To that soft *Charm*, that *Spell*, that *Magick Bough*,
That high Enchantment I betake me now: 10
And to that Hand, (the Branch of Heavens faire Tree)
I kneele for help; O! lay that hand on me,
Adored *Cesar!* and my Faith is such,
I shall be heal'd, if that my KING but touch.
The Evill is not Yours: my sorrow sings,
Mine is the Evill, but the Cure, the KINGS.

Upon Jollies wife

First, *Jollies* wife is lame; then next, loose-hipt:
Squint-ey'd, hook-nos'd; and lastly, Kidney-lipt.

To a Gentlewoman, objecting
to him his gray haires

Am I despis'd, because you say,
And I dare sweare, that I am gray?
Know, Lady, you have but your day:
And time will come when you shall weare
Such frost and snow upon your haire:
And when (though long it comes to passe)
You question with your Looking-glasse;
And in that sincere *Christall* seek,
But find no Rose-bud in your cheek:
Nor any bed to give the shew   10
Where such a rare Carnation grew.
Ah! then too late, close in your chamber keeping,
             It will be told
             That you are old;
By those true teares y'are weeping.

Upon a black Twist, rounding the Arme of the Countesse of Carlile

I saw about her spotlesse wrist,
Of blackest silk, a curious twist;
Which, circumvolving gently, there
Enthrall'd her Arme, as Prisoner.
Dark was the Jayle; but as if light
Had met t'engender with the night;
Or so, as Darknesse made a stay
To shew at once, both night and day.
I fancie none! but if there be
Such Freedome in Captivity;   10
I beg of Love, that ever I
May in like Chains of Darknesse lie.

A Ring presented to Julia

Julia, I bring
To thee this Ring,
Made for thy finger fit;
To shew by this,
That our love is
(Or sho'd be) like to it.

Close though it be,
The joynt is free:
So when Love's yoke is on,
It must not gall,   10
Or fret at all
With hard oppression.

But it must play
Still either way;
And be, too, such a yoke,
As not too wide,
To over-slide;
Or be so strait to choak.

        So we, who beare,
        This beame, must reare   20
Our selves to such a height:
        As that the stay
        Of either may
Create the burden light.

        And as this round
        Is no where found
To flaw, or else to sever:
        So let our love
        As endless prove;
And pure as Gold for ever.   30

Julia's Petticoat

Thy Azure Robe, I did behold,
As ayrie as the leaves of gold;
Which erring here, and wandring there,
Pleas'd with transgression ev'ry where:
Sometimes 'two'd pant, and sigh, and heave,
As if to stir it scarce had leave:
But having got it; thereupon,
'Two'd make a brave expansion.
And pounc't with Stars, it shew'd to me
Like a *Celestiall Canopie*.   10
Sometimes 'two'd blaze, and then abate,
Like to a flame growne moderate:
Sometimes away 'two'd wildly fling;
Then to thy thighs so closely cling,
That some conceit did melt me downe,
As Lovers fall into a swoone:
And all confus'd, I there did lie
Drown'd in Delights; but co'd not die.
That Leading Cloud, I follow'd still,
Hoping t'ave seene of it my fill;   20
But ah! I co'd not: sho'd it move
To Life Eternal, I co'd love.

Get up, get up for shame, the Blooming Morne
Upon her wings presents the god unshorne.
 See how *Aurora* throwes her faire
 Fresh-quilted colours through the aire:
 Get up, sweet-Slug-a-bed, and see
 The Dew-bespangling Herbe and Tree.
Each Flower has wept, and bow'd toward the East,
Above an houre since; yet you not drest,
 Nay! not so much as out of bed?
 When all the Birds have Mattens seyd,   10
 And sung their thankfull Hymnes: 'tis sin,
 Nay, profanation to keep in,
When as a thousand Virgins on this day,
Spring, sooner then the Lark, to fetch in May.

Rise; and put on your Foliage, and be seene
To come forth, like the Spring-time, fresh and greene;
 And sweet as *Flora*. Take no care
 For Jewels for your Gowne, or Haire:
 Feare not; the leaves will strew
 Gemms in abundance upon you: 20
Besides, the childhood of the Day has kept,
Against you come, some *Orient Pearls* unwept:
 Come, and receive them while the light
 Hangs on the Dew-locks of the night:
 And *Titan* on the Eastern hill
 Retires himselfe, or else stands still
Till you come forth. Wash, dresse, be brief in praying:
Few Beads are best, when once we goe a Maying.

Come, my *Corinna*, come; and comming, marke
How each field turns a street; each street a Parke   30
 Made green, and trimm'd with trees: see how
 Devotion gives each House a Bough,
 Or Branch: Each Porch, each doore, ere this,
 An Arke a Tabernacle is
Made up of white-thorn neatly enterwove;
As if here were those cooler shades of love.

Can such delights be in the street,
And open fields, and we not see't?
Come, we'll abroad; and let's obay
The Proclamation made for May: 40
And sin no more, as we have done, by staying;
But my *Corinna*, come, let's goe a Maying.

There's not a budding Boy, or Girle, this day,
But is got up, and gone to bring in May.
A deale of Youth, ere this, is come
Back, and with *White-thorn* laden home.
Some have dispatcht their Cakes and Creame,
Before that we have left to dreame:
And some have wept, and woo'd, and plighted Troth,
And chose their Priest, ere we can cast off sloth: 50
Many a green-gown has been given;
Many a kisse, both odde and even:
Many a glance too has been sent
From out the eye, Loves Firmament:
Many a jest told of the Keyes betraying
This night, and Locks pickt, yet w'are not a Maying.

Come, let us goe, while we are in our prime;
And take the harmlesse follie of the time.
We shall grow old apace, and die
Before we know our liberty. 60
Our life is short; and our dayes run
As fast away as do's the Sunne:
And as a vapour, or a drop of raine
Once lost, can ne'r be found againe:
So when or you or I are made
A fable, song, or fleeting shade;
All love, all liking, all delight
Lies drown'd with us in endlesse night.
Then while time serves, and we are but decaying;
Come, my *Corinna*, come, let's goe a Maying. 70

Upon Batt

Batt he gets children, not for love to reare 'em;
But out of hope his wife might die to beare 'em.

An Ode to Master Endymion Porter, upon his Brothers death

Not all thy flushing Sunnes are set,
       Herrick, as yet:
Nor doth this far-drawn Hemisphere
Frown, and look sullen ev'ry where.
Daies may conclude in nights; and Suns may rest,
    As dead, within the West;
Yet the next Morne, re-guild the fragrant East.

Alas for me! that I have lost
      E'en all almost:
Sunk is my sight; set is my Sun;   10
And all the loome of life undone:
The staffe, the Elme, the prop, the shelt'ring wall
    Whereon my Vine did crawle,
Now, now, blowne downe; needs must the old stock fall.

Yet, *Porter*, while thou keep'st alive,
      In death I thrive:
And like a *Phenix* re-aspire
From out my *Narde*, and Fun'rall fire:
And as I prune my feather'd youth, so I
    Doe mar'l how I co'd die,   20
When I had Thee, my chiefe Preserver, by.

I'm up, I'm up, and blesse that hand,
      Which makes me stand
Now as I doe; and but for thee,
I must confesse, I co'd not be.
The debt is paid: for he who doth resigne
    Thanks to the gen'rous Vine;
Invites fresh Grapes to fill his Presse with Wine.

To his dying Brother,
Master William Herrick

Life of my life, take not so soone thy flight,
But stay the time till we have bade Good night.
Thou hast both Wind and Tide with thee; Thy way
As soone dispatcht is by the Night, as Day.
Let us not then so rudely henceforth goe
Till we have wept, kist, sigh't, shook hands, or so.
There's paine in parting; and a kind of hell,
When once true-lovers take their last Fare-well.
What? shall we two our endlesse leaves take here
Without a sad looke, or a solemne teare?   10
He knowes not Love, that hath not this truth proved,
Love is most loth to leave the thing beloved.
Pay we our Vowes, and goe; yet when we part,
Then, even then, I will bequeath my heart
Into thy loving hands: For Ile keep none
To warme my Breast, when thou my Pulse art gone.
No, here Ile last, and walk (a harmless shade)
About this Urne, wherein thy Dust is laid,
To guard it so, as nothing here shall be
Heavy, to hurt those sacred seeds of thee.   20

How Lillies came white

White though ye be; yet, Lillies, know,
From the first ye were not so:
   But Ile tell ye
   What befell ye;
Cupid and his Mother lay
In a Cloud; while both did play,
He with his pretty finger prest
The rubie niplet of her breast;
Out of the which, the creame of light,
   Like to a Dew,   .   10
   Fell downe on you,
   And made ye white.

On Gelli-flowers begotten

What was't that fell but now
   From that warme kisse of ours?
Look, look, by Love I vow
   They were two *Gelli-flowers.*

Let's kisse, and kisse agen;
   For if so be our closes
Make *Gelli-flowers,* then
   I'm sure they'l fashion *Roses.*

The Lilly in a Christal

You have beheld a smiling *Rose*
   When Virgins hands have drawn
   O'r it a Cobweb-Lawne:
And here, you see, this Lilly shows,
   Tomb'd in a *Christal* stone,
More faire in this transparent case,
   Then when it grew alone;
   And had but single grace.

You see how *Creame* but naked is;
   Nor daunces in the eye   10
   Without a Strawberrie:
Or some fine tincture, like to this,
   Which draws the sight thereto,
More by that wantoning with it;
   Then when the paler hieu
   No mixture did admit.

You see how *Amber* through the streams
   More gently stroaks the sight,
   With some conceal'd delight;
Then when he darts his radiant beams   20
   Into the boundlesse aire:
Where either too much light his worth

Doth all at once impaire,
Or set it little forth.

Put Purple Grapes, or Cherries in-
To Glasse, and they will send
More beauty to commend
Them, from that cleane and subtile skin,
Then if they naked stood,
And had no other pride at all, .   30
But their own flesh and blood,
And tinctures naturall.

Thus Lillie, Rose, Grape, Cherry, Creame,
And Straw-berry do stir
More love, when they transfer
A weak, a soft, a broken beame;
Then if they sho'd discover
At full their proper excellence;
Without some Scean cast over,
To juggle with the sense.   40

Thus let this *Christal'd Lillie* be
A Rule, how far to teach,
Your nakednesse must reach:
And that, no further, then we see
Those glaring colours laid
By Arts wise hand, but to this end
They sho'd obey a shade;
Lest they too far extend.

So though y'are white as Swan, or Snow,
And have the power to move   50
A world of men to love:
Yet, when your Lawns & Silks shal flow;
And that white cloud divide
Into a doubtful Twi-light; then,
Then will your hidden Pride
Raise greater fires in men.

Upon some women

Thou who wilt not love, doe this;
Learne of me what Woman is.
Something made of thred and thrumme;
A meere Botch of all and some.
Pieces, patches, ropes of haire;
In-laid Garbage ev'ry where.
Out-side silk, and out-side Lawne;
Sceanes to cheat us neatly drawne.
False in legs, and false in thighes;
False in breast, teeth, haire, and eyes: 10
False in head, and false enough;
Onely true in shreds and stuffe.

The Welcome to Sack

So soft streams meet, so springs with gladder smiles
Meet after long divorcement by the Iles:
When Love (the child of likenesse) urgeth on
Their Christal natures to an union.
So meet stolne kisses, when the Moonie nights
Call forth fierce Lovers to their wisht Delights:
So *Kings* & *Queens* meet, when Desire convinces
All thoughts, but such as aime at getting Princes,
As I meet thee. Soule of my life, and fame!
Eternall Lamp of Love! whose radiant flame   10
Out-glares the Heav'ns *Osiris**; and thy gleams
Out-shine the splendour of his mid-day beams.
Welcome, O welcome my illustrious Spouse;
Welcome as are the ends unto my Vowes:
I! far more welcome then the happy soile,
The Sea-scourg'd Merchant, after all his toile,
Salutes with tears of joy; when fires betray
The smoakie chimneys of his *Ithaca*.
Where hast thou been so long from my embraces,

*The Sun.

Poore pittyed Exile? Tell me, did thy Graces   20
Flie discontented hence, and for a time
Did rather choose to blesse another clime?
Or went'st thou to this end, the more to move me,
By thy short absence, to desire and love thee?
Why frowns my Sweet? Why won't my Saint confer
Favours on me, her fierce Idolater?
Why are Those Looks, Those Looks the which have been
Time-past so fragrant, sickly now drawn in
Like a dull Twi-light? Tell me; and the fault
Ile expiate with Sulphur, Haire, and Salt: 30
And with the Christal humour of the spring,
Purge hence the guilt, and kill this quarrelling.
Wo't thou not smile, or tell me what's amisse?
Have I been cold to hug thee, too remisse,
Too temp'rate in embracing? Tell me, ha's desire
To thee-ward dy'd i'th'embers, and no fire
Left in this rak't-up Ash-heap, as a mark
To testifie the glowing of a spark?
Have I divorc't thee onely to combine
In hot Adult'ry with another Wine?   40
True, I confesse I left thee, and appeale
'Twas done by me, more to confirme my zeale,
And double my affection on thee; as doe those,
Whose love growes more enflam'd, by being Foes.
But to forsake thee ever, co'd there be
A thought of such like possibilitie?
When thou thy selfe dar'st say, thy Iles shall lack
Grapes, before *Herrick* leaves Canarie Sack.
Thou mak'st me ayrie, active to be born,
Like *Iphyclus*, upon the tops of Corn.   50
Thou mak'st me nimble, as the winged howers,
To dance and caper on the heads of flowers,
And ride the Sun-beams. Can there be a thing
Under the heavenly *Isis**, that can bring
More love unto my life, or can present
My *Genius* with a fuller blandishment?
Illustrious Idoll! co'd th'*Ægyptians* seek

*The Moon.

Help from the *Garlick, Onyon,* and the *Leek,*
And pay no vowes to thee? who wast their best
God, and far more transcendent then the rest?   60
Had *Cassius,* that weak Water-drinker, known
Thee in thy Vine, or had but tasted one
Small Chalice of thy frantick liquor; He
As the wise *Cato* had approv'd of thee.
Had not *Joves** son, that brave *Tyrinthian* Swain,
(Invited to the *Thesbian banquet*) ta'ne
Full goblets of thy gen'rous blood; his spright
Ne'r had kept heat for fifty Maids that night.
Come, come, and kisse me; Love and lust commends
Thee, and thy beauties; kisse, we will be friends   70
Too strong for Fate to break us: Look upon
Me, with that full pride of complexion,
As *Queenes,* meet *Queenes;* or come thou unto me,
As *Cleopatra* came to *Anthonie;*
When her high carriage did at once present
To the *Triumvir,* Love and Wonderment.
Swell up my nerves with spirit; let my blood
Run through my veines, like to a hasty flood.
Fill each part full of fire, active to doe
What thy commanding soule shall put it to.   80
And till I turne Apostate to thy love,
Which here I vow to serve, doe not remove
Thy Fiers from me; but *Apollo's* curse
Blast these-like actions, or a thing that's worse;
When these Circumstants shall but live to see
The time that I prevaricate from thee.
Call me *The sonne of Beere,* and then confine
Me to the Tap, the Tost, the Turfe; Let Wine
Ne'r shine upon me; May my Numbers all
Run to a sudden Death, and Funerall.   90
And last, when thee (deare Spouse) I disavow,
Ne'r may Prophetique *Daphne* crown my Brow.

   *Hercules.

Impossibilities to his friend

My faithful friend, if you can see
The Fruit to grow up, or the Tree:
If you can see the colour come
Into the blushing Peare, or Plum:
If you can see the water grow
To cakes of Ice, or flakes of Snow:
If you can see, that drop of raine
Lost in the wild sea, once againe:
If you can see, how Dreams do creep
Into the Brain by easie sleep: 10
Then there is hope that you may see
Her love me once, who now hates me.

Upon Luggs. Epig.

Luggs, by the Condemnation of the Bench,
Was lately whipt for lying with a Wench.
Thus Paines and Pleasures turne by turne succeed:
He smarts at last, who do's not first take heed.

Upon Gubbs. Epig.

Gubbs call's his children *Kitlings*: and wo'd bound
(Some say) for joy, to see those Kitlings drown'd.

To live merrily, and to trust to Good Verses

Now is the time for mirth,
  Nor cheek, or tongue be dumbe:
For with the flowrie earth,
  The golden pomp is come.

The golden Pomp is come;
   For now each tree do's weare
(Made of her Pap and Gum)
   Rich beads of *Amber* here.

Now raignes the *Rose*, and now
   Th'*Arabian* Dew besmears
My uncontrolled brow,
   And my retorted haires.

Homer, this Health to thee,
   In Sack of such a kind,
That it wo'd make thee see,
   Though thou wert ne'r so blind.

Next, *Virgil*, Ile call forth,
   To pledge this second Health
In Wine, whose each cup's worth
   An Indian Common-wealth.

A Goblet next Ile drink
   To *Ovid;* and suppose,
Made he the pledge, he'd think
   The world had all *one Nose*.

Then this immensive cup
   Of *Aromatike* wine,
Catullus, I quaffe up
   To that Terce Muse of thine.

Wild I am now with heat;
   O *Bacchus!* coole thy Raies!
Or frantick I shall eate
   Thy *Thyrse*, and bite the *Bayes*.

Round, round, the roof do's run;
   And being ravisht thus,
Come, I will drink a Tun
   To my *Propertius*.

10

20

30

Now, to *Tibullus*, next,
    This flood I drink to thee:
But stay; I see a Text,
    That this presents to me.   40

Behold, *Tibullus* lies
    Here burnt, whose smal return
Of ashes, scarce suffice
    To fill a little Urne.

Trust to good Verses then;
    They onely will aspire,
When Pyramids, as men,
    Are lost, i'th'funerall fire.

And when all Bodies meet
    In *Lethe* to be drown'd;   50
Then onely Numbers sweet,
    With endless life are crown'd.

To the Fever, not to trouble Julia

Th'ast dar'd too farre; but Furie now forbeare
To give the least disturbance to her haire:
But lesse presume to lay a Plait upon
Her skins most smooth, and cleare expansion.
'Tis like a Lawnie-Firmament as yet
Quite dispossest of either fray, or fret.
Come thou not neere that Filmne so finely spred,
Where no one piece is yet unlevelled.
This if thou dost, woe to thee Furie, woe,
Ile send such Frost, such Haile, such Sleet, and Snow,
Such Flesh-quakes, Palsies, and such fears as shall   11
Dead thee to th'most, if not destroy thee all.
And thou a thousand thousand times shalt be
More shak't thy selfe, then she is scorch't by thee.

To Violets

1. Welcome Maids of Honour,
        You doe bring
        In the Spring;
    And wait upon her.

2. She has Virgins many,
        Fresh and faire;
        Yet you are
    More sweet then any.

3. Y'are the Maiden Posies,
        And so grac't,   10
        To be plac't,
    'Fore Damask Roses.

4. Yet though thus respected,
        By and by
        Ye doe lie,
    Poore Girles, neglected.

Upon Bunce. Epig.

Mony thou ow'st me; Prethee fix a day
For payment promis'd, though thou never pay:
Let it be Doomes-day; nay, take longer scope;
Pay when th'art honest; let me have some hope.

To the Virgins, to make much of Time

1. Gather ye Rose-buds while ye may,
        Old Time is still a flying:
    And this same flower that smiles to day,
        To morrow will be dying.

    [*To the Virgins, to make much of Time*]   63

2. The glorious Lamp of Heaven, the Sun,
        The higher he's a getting;
   The sooner will his Race be run,
        And neerer he's to Setting.

3. That Age is best, which is the first,
        When Youth and Blood are warmer;   10
   But being spent, the worse, and worst
        Times, still succeed the former.

4. Then be not coy, but use your time;
        And while ye may, goe marry:
   For having lost but once your prime,
        You may for ever tarry.

His Poetrie his Pillar

1. Onely a little more
        I have to write,
        Then Ile give o're,
   And bid the world Good-night.

2. 'Tis but a flying minute,
        That I must stay,
        Or linger in it;
   And then I must away.

3. O time that cut'st down all!
        And scarce leav'st here
        Memoriall
   Of any men that were.

4. How many lye forgot
        In Vaults beneath?
        And piece-meale rot
   Without a fame in death?

5. Behold this living stone,
     I reare for me,
     Ne'r to be thrown
Downe, envious Time by thee.   20

6. Pillars let some set up,
     (If so they please)
     Here is my hope,
And my *Pyramides*.

Safety on the Shore

What though the sea be calme? Trust to the shore:
Ships have been drown'd, where late they danc't before.

To the Lark

Good speed, for I this day
Betimes my Mattens say:
  Because I doe
  Begin to wooe:
  Sweet singing Lark,
  Be thou the Clark,
  And know thy when
  To say, *Amen*.
  And if I prove
  Blest in my love;   10
  Then thou shalt be
  High-Priest to me,
  At my returne,
  To Incense burne;
And so to solemnize
Love's, and my Sacrifice.

A Meditation for his Mistresse

1. You are a *Tulip* seen to day,
   But (Dearest) of so short a stay;
   That where you grew, scarce man can say.

2. You are a lovely *July-flower*,
   Yet one rude wind, or ruffling shower,
   Will force you hence, (and in an houre.)

3. You are a sparkling *Rose* i'th'bud,
   Yet lost, ere that chast flesh and blood
   Can shew where you or grew, or stood.

4. You are a full-spread faire-set Vine,   10
   And can with Tendrills love intwine,
   Yet dry'd, ere you distill your Wine.

5. You are like Balme inclosed (well)
   In *Amber*, or some *Chrystall* shell,
   Yet lost ere you transfuse your smell.

6. You are a dainty *Violet*,
   Yet wither'd, ere you can be set
   Within the Virgins Coronet.

7. You are the *Queen* all flowers among,
   But die you must (faire Maid) ere long,   20
   As He, the maker of this Song.

Lyrick for Legacies

Gold I've none, for use or show,
Neither Silver to bestow
At my death; but thus much know,
That each Lyrick here shall be
Of my love a Legacie,

Left to all posterity.
Gentle friends, then doe but please,
To accept such coynes as these;
As my last Remembrances.

Great boast, small rost

Of Flanks and Chines of Beefe doth *Gorrell* boast
He has at home; but who tasts boil'd or rost?
Look in his Brine-tub, and you shall find there
Two stiffe-blew-Pigs-feet, and a sow's cleft eare.

The Fairie Temple: or, Oberons Chappell

DEDICATED TO MR. JOHN MERRIFIELD,
COUNSELLOR AT LAW

Rare Temples thou hast seen, I know,
And rich for in and outward show:
Survey this Chappell, built, alone,
Without or Lime, or Wood, or Stone:
Then say, if one th'ast seene more fine
Then this, the Fairies once, now *Thine*.

THE TEMPLE

A way enchac't with glasse & beads
There is, that to the Chappel leads:
Whose structure (for his holy rest)
Is here the *Halcion's* curious nest: 10
Into the which who looks shall see
His *Temple of Idolatry*:
Where he of *God-heads* has such store,
As *Rome's Pantheon* had not more.
His house of *Rimmon*, this he calls,
Girt with small bones, instead of walls.
First, in a *Neech,* more black then jet,

His Idol-Cricket there is set:
Then in a Polisht Ovall by
There stands his *Idol-Beetle-flie:*   20
Next in an Arch, akin to this,
His *Idol-Canker* seated is:
Then in a Round, is plac't by these,
His golden god, *Cantharides.*
So that where ere ye look, ye see,
No *Capitoll,* no *Cornish* free,
Or *Freeze,* from this fine Fripperie.
Now this the Fairies wo'd have known,
Theirs is a mixt Religion.
And some have heard the Elves it call   30
Part Pagan, part Papisticall.
If unto me all Tongues were granted,
I co'd not speak the Saints here painted.
Saint *Tit,* Saint *Nit,* Saint *Is,* Saint *Itis,*
Who 'gainst *Mabs-state* plac't here right is.
Saint *Will o'th'Wispe* (of no great bignes)
But *alias* call'd here *Fatuus ignis.*
Saint *Frip,* Saint *Trip,* Saint *Fill,* S. *Fillie,*
Neither those other-Saint-ships will I
Here goe about for to recite   40
Their number (almost) infinite,
Which one by one here set downe are
In this most curious Calendar.
First, at the entrance of the gate,
A little-Puppet-Priest doth wait,
Who squeaks to all the commers there,
Favour your tongues, who enter here.
Pure hands bring hither, without staine.
A second pules, *Hence, hence, profane.*
Hard by, i'th'shell of halfe a nut,   50
The Holy-water there is put:
A little brush of Squirrils haires,
(Compos'd of odde, not even paires)
Stands in the Platter, or close by,
To purge the Fairie Family.
Neere to the Altar stands the Priest,
There off'ring up the Holy-Grist:

[*The Fairie Temple: or, Oberons Chappell*]   68

Ducking in Mood, and perfect Tense,
With (much-good-do't him) reverence.
The Altar is not here foure-square, 60
Nor in a forme Triangular;
Nor made of glasse, or wood, or stone,
But of a little Transverce bone;
Which boyes, and Bruckel'd children call
(Playing for Points and Pins) *Cockall*.
Whose Linnen-Drapery is a thin
Subtile and ductile Codlin's skin;
Which o're the board is smoothly spred,
With little Seale-work Damasked.
The Fringe that circumbinds it too, 70
Is Spangle-work of trembling dew,
Which, gently gleaming, makes a show,
Like Frost-work glitt'ring on the Snow.
Upon this fetuous board doth stand
Something for *Shew-bread*, and at hand
(Just in the middle of the Altar)
Upon an end, the *Fairie-Psalter*,
Grac't with the Trout-flies curious wings,
Which serve for watched Ribbanings.
Now, we must know, the Elves are led 80
Right by the Rubrick, which they read.
And if Report of them be true,
They have their Text for what they doe;
I, and their Book of Canons too.
And, as Sir *Thomas Parson* tells,
They have their Book of Articles:
And if that Fairie Knight not lies,
They have their Book of Homilies:
And other Scriptures, that designe
A short, but righteous discipline. 90
The Bason stands the board upon
To take the Free-Oblation:
A little Pin-dust; which they hold
More precious, then we prize our gold:
Which charity they give to many
Poore of the Parish, (if there's any)
Upon the ends of these neat Railes

(Hatcht, with the Silver-light of snails)
The Elves, in formall manner, fix
Two pure, and holy *Candlesticks:*　　　　　　　100
In either which a small tall bent
Burns for the Altars ornament.
For sanctity, they have, to these,
Their curious *Copes* and *Surplices*
Of cleanest *Cobweb,* hanging by
In their *Religious Vesterie.*
They have their *Ash-pans,* & their *Brooms*
To purge the Chappel and the rooms:
Their many *mumbling Masse-priests* here,
And many a dapper *Chorister.*　　　　　　　110
Their ush'ring *Vergers,* here likewise,
Their *Canons,* and their *Chaunteries:*
Of *Cloyster-Monks* they have enow,
I, and their *Abby-Lubbers* too:
And if their Legend doe not lye,
They much affect the *Papacie:*
And since the last is dead, there's hope,
Elve Boniface shall next be Pope.
They have their *Cups* and *Chalices;*
Their *Pardons* and *Indulgences:*　　　　　　120
Their *Beads* of Nits, *Bels, Books, & Wax*
Candles (forsooth) and other knacks:
Their *Holy Oyle,* their *Fasting-Spittle;*
Their *sacred Salt* here, (not a little.)
Dry *chips,* old *shooes, rags, grease, & bones;*
Beside their *Fumigations,*
To drive the Devill from the Cod-piece
Of the Fryar, (of work an odde-piece.)
Many a trifle too, and trinket,
And for what use, scarce man wo'd think it.　　130
Next, then, upon the *Chanters* side
An *Apples-core* is hung up dry'd,
With ratling Kirnils, which is rung
To call to Morn, and Even-Song.
The Saint, to which the most he prayes
And offers *Incense* Nights and dayes,
The *Lady* of the *Lobster* is,

Whose foot-pace he doth stroak & kisse;
And, humbly, chives of Saffron brings,
For his most cheerfull offerings.   140
When, after these, h'as paid his vows,
He lowly to the Altar bows:
And then he dons the Silk-worms shed,
(Like a *Turks Turbant* on his head)
And reverently departeth thence,
Hid in a cloud of *Frankincense:*
And by the glow-worms light wel guided,
Goes to the Feast that's now provided.

To Musique, to becalme his Fever

1. Charm me asleep, and melt me so
          With thy Delicious Numbers;
   That being ravisht, hence I goe
          Away in easie slumbers.
             Ease my sick head,
             And make my bed,
   Thou Power that canst sever
             From me this ill:
             And quickly still:
             Though thou not kill   10
                My Fever.

2. Thou sweetly canst convert the same
          From a consuming fire,
   Into a gentle-licking flame,
          And make it thus expire.
             Then make me weep
             My paines asleep;
   And give me such reposes,
             That I, poore I,
             May think, thereby,   20
             I live and die
                'Mongst Roses.

3. Fall on me like a silent dew,
        Or like those Maiden showrs,
    Which, by the peepe of day, doe strew
        A Baptime o're the flowers.
        Melt, melt my paines,
        With thy soft straines;
    That having ease me given,
        With full delight,
        I leave this light;
        And take my flight
            For Heaven.

30

No Lock against Letcherie

Barre close as you can, and bolt fast too your doore,
To keep out the Letcher, and keep in the whore:
Yet, quickly you'l see by the turne of a pin,
The Whore to come out, or the Letcher come in.

Neglect

Art quickens Nature; Care will make a face:
Neglected beauty perisheth apace.

Upon himselfe

Mop-ey'd I am, as some have said,
Because I've liv'd so long a maid:
But grant that I sho'd wedded be,
Sho'd I a jot the better see?
No, I sho'd think, that Marriage might,
Rather then mend, put out the light.

Upon Sudds a Laundresse

Sudds Launders Bands in pisse; and starches them
Both with her Husband's, and her own tough fleame.

To his Booke

Thou art a plant sprung up to wither never,
But like a Laurell, to grow green for ever.

Upon a crooked Maid

Crooked you are, but that dislikes not me;
So you be straight, where Virgins straight sho'd be.

Draw Gloves

At Draw-Gloves we'l play,
   And prethee, let's lay
A wager, and let it be this;
   Who first to the Summe
   Of twenty shall come,
Shall have for his winning a kisse.

The Hock-cart, or Harvest home

TO THE RIGHT HONOURABLE, MILDMAY,
EARLE OF WESTMORLAND

Come Sons of Summer, by whose toile,
We are the Lords of Wine and Oile;
By whose tough labours, and rough hands,
We rip up first, then reap our lands.

Crown'd with the eares of corne, now come,
And, to the Pipe, sing Harvest home.
Come forth, my Lord, and see the Cart
Drest up with all the Country Art.
See, here a *Maukin*, there a sheet,
As spotlesse pure, as it is sweet: 10
The Horses, Mares, and frisking Fillies,
(Clad, all, in Linnen, white as Lillies.)
The Harvest Swaines, and Wenches bound
For joy, to see the *Hock-cart* crown'd.
About the Cart, heare, how the Rout
Of Rurall Younglings raise the shout;
Pressing before, some coming after,
Those with a shout, and these with laughter.
Some blesse the Cart; some kisse the sheaves;
Some prank them up with Oaken leaves: 20
Some crosse the Fill-horse; some with great
Devotion, stroak the home-borne wheat:
While other Rusticks, lesse attent
To Prayers, then to Merryment,
Run after with their breeches rent.
Well, on, brave boyes, to your Lords Hearth,
Glitt'ring with fire; where, for your mirth,
Ye shall see first the large and cheefe
Foundation of your Feast, Fat Beefe:
With Upper Stories, Mutton, Veale   30
And Bacon, (which makes full the meale)
With sev'rall dishes standing by,
As here a Custard, there a Pie,
And here all tempting Frumentie.
And for to make the merry cheere,
If smirking Wine be wanting here,
There's that, which drowns all care, stout Beere;
Which freely drink to your Lords health,
Then to the Plough, (the Common-wealth)
Next to your Flailes, your Fanes, your Fatts;   40
Then to the Maids with Wheaten Hats:
To the rough Sickle, and crookt Sythe,
Drink frollick boyes, till all be blythe.
Feed, and grow fat; and as ye eat,

Be mindfull, that the lab'ring Neat
(As you) may have their fill of meat.
And know, besides, ye must revoke
The patient Oxe unto the Yoke,
And all goe back unto the Plough
And Harrow, (though they'r hang'd up now.)   50
And, you must know, your Lords word's true,
Feed him ye must, whose food fils you.
And that this pleasure is like raine,
Not sent ye for to drowne your paine,
But for to make it spring againe.

Not to love

He that will not love, must be
My Scholar, and learn this of me:
There be in Love as many feares,
As the Summers Corne has eares:
Sighs, and sobs, and sorrowes more
Then the sand, that makes the shore:
Freezing cold, and firie heats,
Fainting swoones, and deadly sweats;
Now an Ague, then a Fever,
Both tormenting Lovers ever.   10
Wod'st thou know, besides all these,
How hard a woman 'tis to please?
How crosse, how sullen, and how soone
She shifts and changes like the Moone.
How false, how hollow she's in heart;
And how she is her owne least part:
How high she's priz'd, and worth but small;
Little thou't love, or not at all.

How Roses came red

1. Roses at first were white,
        Till they co'd not agree,

Whether my *Sapho*'s breast,
　　　Or they more white sho'd be.

2. But being vanquisht quite,
　　　A blush their cheeks bespred;
Since which (beleeve the rest)
　　　The *Roses* first came red.

Upon Groynes. Epig.

Groynes, for his fleshly *Burglary* of late,
Stood in the *Holy-Forum Candidate:*
The word is *Roman;* but in English knowne:
Penance, and standing so, are both but one.

To the Willow-tree

1. Thou art to all lost love the best,
　　　The onely true plant found,
Wherewith young men and maids distrest,
　　　And left of love, are crown'd.

2. When once the Lovers Rose is dead,
　　　Or laid aside forlorne;
Then Willow-garlands, 'bout the head,
　　　Bedew'd with teares, are worne.

3. When with Neglect, (the Lovers bane)
　　　Poore Maids rewarded be,
For their love lost; their onely gaine
　　　Is but a Wreathe from thee.   10

4. And underneath thy cooling shade,
　　　(When weary of the light)
The love-spent Youth, and love-sick Maid,
　　　Come to weep out the night.

The Poets good wishes for the most hopefull and handsome Prince, the Duke of Yorke

May his pretty Duke-ship grow
Like t'a Rose of *Jericho*:
Sweeter far, then ever yet
Showrs or Sun-shines co'd beget.
May the Graces, and the Howers
Strew his hopes, and Him with flowers:
And so dresse him up with Love,
As to be the Chick of *Jove*.
May the thrice-three-Sisters sing
Him the Soveraigne of their Spring: 10
And entitle none to be
Prince of *Hellicon*, but He.
May his soft foot, where it treads,
Gardens thence produce and Meads:
And those Meddowes full be set
With the Rose, and Violet.
May his ample Name be knowne
To the last succession:
And his actions high be told
Through the world, but writ in gold.   20

More potent, lesse peccant

He that may sin, sins least; Leave to transgresse
Enfeebles much the seeds of wickednesse.

To Meddowes

1. Ye have been fresh and green,
        Ye have been fill'd with flowers:
    And ye the Walks have been
        Where Maids have spent their houres.

2. You have beheld, how they
       With *Wicker Arks* did come
   To kisse, and beare away
       The richer Couslips home.

3. Y'ave heard them sweetly sing,
       And seen them in a Round: 10
   Each Virgin, like a Spring,
       With Hony-succles crown'd.

4. But now, we see, none here,
       Whose silv'rie feet did tread,
   And with dishevell'd Haire,
       Adorn'd this smoother Mead.

5. Like Unthrifts, having spent,
       Your stock, and needy grown,
   Y'are left here to lament
       Your poore estates, alone.   20

A Nuptiall Song, or Epithalamie,
on Sir Clipseby Crew and his Lady

1. What's that we see from far? the spring of Day
Bloom'd from the East, or faire Injewel'd May
       Blowne out of April; or some New-
       Star fill'd with glory to our view,
               Reaching at heaven,
   To adde a nobler Planet to the seven?
               Say, or doe we not descrie
   Some Goddesse, in a cloud of Tiffanie
               To move, or rather the
       Emergent *Venus* from the Sea?   10

2. 'Tis she! 'tis she! or else some more Divine
Enlightned substance; mark how from the Shrine
       Of holy Saints she paces on,
       Treading upon *Vermilion*
               And *Amber*; Spice-

ing the Chafte Aire with fumes of Paradise.
   Then come on, come on, and yeeld
A savour like unto a blessed field,
    When the bedabled Morne
    Washes the golden eares of corne.   20

3. See where she comes; and smell how all the street
Breathes Vine-yards and Pomgranats: O how sweet!
    As a fir'd Altar, is each stone,
    Perspiring pounded Cynamon.
     The Phenix nest,
Built up of odours, burneth in her breast.
    Who therein wo'd not consume
His soule to Ash-heaps in that rich perfume?
     Bestroaking Fate the while
    He burnes to Embers on the Pile.   30

4. *Himen, O Himen!* Tread the sacred ground;
Shew thy white feet, and head with Marjoram crown'd:
    Mount up thy flames, and let thy Torch
    Display the Bridegroom in the porch,
     In his desires
More towring, more disparkling then thy fires:
    Shew her how his eyes do turne
And roule about, and in their motions burne
     Their balls to Cindars: haste,
    Or else to ashes he will waste.   40

5. Glide by the banks of Virgins then, and passé
The Shewers of Roses, lucky-foure-leav'd grasse:
    The while the cloud of younglings sing,
    And drown yee with a flowrie Spring:
     While some repeat
Your praise, and bless you, sprinkling you with Wheat:
    While that others doe divine;
Blest is the Bride, on whom the Sun doth shine;
     And thousands gladly wish
    You multiply, as doth a Fish.   50

6. And beautious Bride we do confess y'are wise,

    [A *Nuptiall Song, or Epithalamie*] 79

In dealing forth these bashfull jealousies:
>> In Lov's name do so; and a price
>> Set on your selfe, by being nice:
>>> But yet take heed;
What now you seem, be not the same indeed,
>> And turne *Apostate:* Love will
Part of the way be met; or sit stone-still.
>>> On then, and though you slow-
>> ly go, yet, howsoever, go.   60

7. And now y'are enter'd; see the Codled Cook
Runs from his *Torrid Zone,* to prie, and look,
>> And blesse his dainty Mistresse: see,
>> The Aged point out, This is she,
>>> Who now must sway
The House (Love shield her) with her Yea and Nay:
>> And the smirk Butler thinks it
Sin, in's Nap'rie, not to express his wit;
>>> Each striving to devise
>> Some gin, wherewith to catch your eyes.   70

8. To bed, to bed, kind Turtles, now, and write
This the short'st day, and this the longest night;
>> But yet too short for you: 'tis we,
>> Who count this night as long as three,
>>> Lying alone,
Telling the Clock strike Ten, Eleven, Twelve, One.
>> Quickly, quickly then prepare;
And let the Young-men and the Bride-maids share
>>> Your Garters; and their joynts
>> Encircle with the Bride-grooms Points.   80

9. By the Brides eyes, and by the teeming life
Of her green hopes, we charge ye, that no strife
>> (Farther then Gentlenes tends) gets place
>> Among ye, striving for her lace:
>>> O doe not fall
Foule in these noble pastimes, lest ye call
>> Discord in, and so divide
The youthfull Bride-groom, and the fragrant Bride:

>> *[A Nuptiall Song, or Epithalamie]*   80

Which Love fore-fend; but spoken,
Be't to your praise, no peace was broken.   90

10. Strip her of Spring-time, tender-whimpring-maids,
Now *Autumne's* come, when all those flowrie aids
Of her Delayes must end; Dispose
That *Lady-smock*, that *Pansie*, and that *Rose*
Neatly apart;
But for *Prick-madam*, and for *Gentle-heart;*
And soft-*Maidens-blush*, the Bride
Makes holy these, all others lay aside:
Then strip her, or unto her
Let him come, who dares undo her.   100

11. And to enchant yee more, see every where
About the Roofe a *Syren* in a Sphere;
(As we think) singing to the dinne
Of many a warbling *Cherubin:*
O marke yee how
The soule of Nature melts in numbers: now
See, a thousand *Cupids* flye,
To light their Tapers at the Brides bright eye.
To Bed; or her they'l tire,
Were she an Element of fire.   110

12. And to your more bewitching, see, the proud
Plumpe Bed beare up, and swelling like a cloud,
Tempting the too too modest; can
Yee see it brusle like a Swan,
And you be cold
To meet it, when it woo's and seemes to fold
The Armes to hugge you? throw, throw
Your selves into the mighty over-flow
Of that white Pride, and Drowne
The night, with you, in floods of Downe.   120

13. The bed is ready, and the maze of Love
Lookes for the treaders; every where is wove
Wit and new misterie; read, and
Put in practise, to understand

[*A Nuptiall Song, or Epithalamie*]   81

And know each wile,
Each hieroglyphick of a kisse or smile;
And do it to the full; reach
High in your own conceipt, and some way teach
Nature and Art, one more
Play, then they ever knew before.   130

14. If needs we must for Ceremonies-sake,
Blesse a *Sack-posset*; Luck go with it; take
The Night-Charme quickly; you have spells,
And magicks for to end, and hells,
To passe; but such
And of such Torture as no one would grutch
To live therein for ever: Frie
And consume, and grow again to die,
And live, and in that case,
Love the confusion of the place.   140

15. But since It must be done, dispatch, and sowe
Up in a sheet your Bride, and what if so
It be with Rock, or walles of Brasse,
Ye Towre her up, as *Danae* was;
Think you that this,
Or hell it selfe a powerfull Bulwarke is?
I tell yee no; but like a
Bold bolt of thunder he will make his way,
And rend the cloud, and throw
The sheet about, like flakes of snow.   150

16. All now is husht in silence; *Midwife-moone*,
With all her *Owle-ey'd* issue begs a boon
Which you must grant; that's entrance; with
Which extract, all we can call pith
And quintiscence
Of Planetary bodies; so commence
All faire *Constellations*
Looking upon yee, that two Nations
Springing from two such Fires,
May blaze the vertue of their Sires.   160

[*A Nuptiall Song, or Epithalamie*]   82

The silken Snake

For sport my *Julia* threw a Lace
Of silke and silver at my face:
Watchet the silke was; and did make
A shew, as if't'ad been a snake:
The suddenness did me affright;
But though it scar'd, it did not bite.

Upon Shark. Epig.

Shark, when he goes to any publick feast,
Eates to ones thinking, of all there, the least.
What saves the master of the House thereby?
When if the servants search, they may descry
In his wide Codpeece, (dinner being done)
Two Napkins cram'd up, and a silver Spoone.

Oberons Feast

Shapcot! To thee the Fairy State
I with discretion, dedicate.
Because thou prizest things that are
Curious, and un-familiar.
Take first the feast; these dishes gone;
Wee'l see the Fairy-Court anon.

A little mushroome table spred,
After short prayers, they set on bread;
A Moon-parcht grain of purest wheat,
With some small glit'ring gritt, to eate
His choyce bitts with; then in a trice
They make a feast lesse great then nice.
But all this while his eye is serv'd,
We must not thinke his eare was sterv'd:

10

But that there was in place to stir
His Spleen, the chirring Grashopper;
The merry Cricket, puling Flie,
The piping Gnat for minstralcy.
And now, we must imagine first,
The Elves present to quench his thirst   20
A pure seed-Pearle of Infant dew,
Brought and besweetned in a blew
And pregnant violet; which done,
His kitling eyes begin to runne
Quite through the table, where he spies
The hornes of paperie Butterflies,
Of which he eates, and tastes a little
Of that we call the Cuckoes spittle.
A little Fuz-ball-pudding stands
By, yet not blessed by his hands,   30
That was too coorse; but then forthwith
He ventures boldly on the pith
Of sugred Rush, and eates the sagge
And well bestrutted Bees sweet bagge:
Gladding his pallat with some store
Of Emits eggs; what wo'd he more?
But Beards of Mice, a Newt's stew'd thigh,
A bloated Earewig, and a Flie;
With the Red-capt worme, that's shut
Within the concave of a Nut,   40
Browne as his Tooth. A little Moth,
Late fatned in a piece of cloth:
With withered cherries; Mandrakes eares;
Moles eyes; to these, the slain-Stags teares:
The unctuous dewlaps of a Snaile;
The broke-heart of a Nightingale
Ore-come in musicke; with a wine,
Ne're ravisht from the flattering Vine,
But gently prest from the soft side
Of the most sweet and dainty Bride,   50
Brought in a dainty daizie, which
He fully quaffs up to bewitch
His blood to height; this done, commended
Grace by his Priest; *The feast is ended.*

Upon a child that dyed

Here she lies, a pretty bud,
Lately made of flesh and blood:
Who, as soone, fell fast asleep,
As her little eyes did peep.
Give her strewings; but not stir
The earth, that lightly covers her.

To Daffadills

1. Faire Daffadills, we weep to see
        You haste away so soone:
    As yet the early-rising Sun
        Has not attain'd his Noone.
            Stay, stay,
        Untill the hasting day
            Has run
        But to the Even-song;
    And, having pray'd together, we
        Will goe with you along.   10

2. We have short time to stay, as you,
        We have as short a Spring;
    As quick a growth to meet Decay,
        As you, or any thing.
            We die,
        As your hours doe, and drie
            Away,
        Like to the Summers raine;
    Or as the pearles of Mornings dew
        Ne'r to be found againe.   20

The Christian Militant

A man prepar'd against all ills to come,
That dares to dead the fire of martirdome:
That sleeps at home; and sayling there at ease,

[The Christian Militant] 85

Feares not the fierce sedition of the Seas:
That's counter-proofe against the Farms mis-haps,
Undreadfull too of courtly thunderclaps:
That weares one face (like heaven) and never showes
A change, when Fortune either comes, or goes:
That keepes his own strong guard, in the despight
Of what can hurt by day, or harme by night: 10
That takes and re-delivers every stroake
Of Chance, (as made up all of rock, and oake:)
That sighs at others death; smiles at his own
Most dire and horrid crucifixion.
Who for true glory suffers thus; we grant
Him to be here our *Christian militant*.

His embalming to Julia

For my embalming, *Julia,* do but this,
Give thou my lips but their supreamest kiss:
Or else trans-fuse thy breath into the chest,
Where my small reliques must for ever rest:
That breath the *Balm,* the *myrrh,* the *Nard* shal be,
To give an *incorruption* unto me.

The Kisse. A Dialogue.

  1. Among thy Fancies, tell me this,
     What is the thing we call a kisse?
  2. I shall resolve ye, what it is.

     It is a creature born and bred
     Between the lips, (all cherrie-red,)
     By love and warme desires fed,
CHOR. And makes more soft the Bridall bed.

  2. It is an active flame, that flies,
     First, to the Babies of the eyes;

And charmes them there with lullabies;   10
CHOR. And stils the Bride too, when she cries.

2. Then to the chin, the cheek, the eare,
   It frisks, and flyes, now here, now there,
   'Tis now farre off, and then tis nere; /
CHOR. And here, and there, and every where.

1. Ha's it a speaking virtue? 2. Yes;
1. How speaks it, say? 2. Do you but this,
   Part your joyn'd lips, then speaks your kisse;
CHOR. And this loves sweetest language is.

1. Has it a body? 2. I, and wings   20
   With thousand rare encolourings:
   And as it flyes, it gently sings,
CHOR. Love, honie yeelds; but never stings.

To Larr

No more shall I, since I am driven hence,
Devote to thee my graines of Frankinsence:
No more shall I from mantle-trees hang downe,
To honour thee, my little Parsly crown:
No more shall I (I feare me) to thee bring
My chives of Garlick for an offering:
No more shall I, from henceforth, heare a quire
Of merry Crickets by my Country fire.
Go where I will, thou luckie *Larr* stay here,
Warme by a glit'ring chimnie all the yeare.   10

The departure of the good Daemon

What can I do in Poetry,
Now the good Spirit's gone from me?
Why nothing now, but lonely sit,
And over-read what I have writ.

Upon his Julia

Will ye heare, what I can say
Briefly of my *Julia*?
Black and rowling is her eye,
Double chinn'd, and forehead high:
Lips she has, all Rubie red,
Cheeks like Creame Enclarited:
And a nose that is the grace
And *Proscenium* of her face.
So that we may guesse by these,
The other parts will richly please.   10

To my ill Reader

Thou say'st my lines are hard;
   And I the truth will tell;
They are both hard, and marr'd,
   If thou not read'st them well.

Her Bed

See'st thou that Cloud as silver cleare,
Plump, soft, & swelling every where?
Tis *Julia's* Bed, and she sleeps there.

Her Legs

Fain would I kiss my *Julia's* dainty Leg,
Which is as white and hair-less as an egge.

Long and Lazie

That was the Proverb. Let my mistresse be
Lasie to others, but be long to me.

Chop-Cherry

1. Thou gav'st me leave to kisse;
   Thou gav'st me leave to wooe;
   Thou mad'st me thinke by this,
   And that, thou lov'dst me too.

2. But I shall ne'r forget,
   How for to make thee merry;
   Thou mad'st me chop, but yet,
   Another snapt the Cherry.

His Lachrimae or Mirth, turn'd to mourning

1.   Call me no more,
         As heretofore,
   The musick of a Feast;
         Since now (alas)
         The mirth, that was
   In me, is dead or ceast.

2.   Before I went
         To banishment
   Into the loathed West;
         I co'd rehearse
         A Lyrick verse,
   And speak it with the best.

10

3.   But time (Ai me)
         Has laid, I see

[His Lachrimæ or Mirth, turn'd to mourning]   89

My Organ fast asleep;
    And turn'd my voice
    Into the noise
Of those that sit and weep.

Upon his kinswoman Mistris Elizabeth Herrick

Sweet virgin, that I do not set
The pillars up of weeping *Jet,*
Or mournfull *Marble;* let thy shade
Not wrathfull seem, or fright the Maide,
Who hither at her wonted howers
Shall come to strew thy earth with flowers.
No, know (Blest Maide) when there's not one
Remainder left of Brasse or stone,
Thy living Epitaph shall be,
Though lost in them, yet found in me.   10
Dear, in thy *bed of Roses,* then,
Till this world shall dissolve as men,
Sleep, while we hide thee from the light,
Drawing thy curtains round: *Good night.*

To his Valentine, on S. Valentines day

Oft have I heard both Youths and Virgins say,
Birds chuse their Mates, and couple too, this day:
But by their flight I never can divine,
When I shall couple with my Valentine.

Upon M. Ben. Johnson. Epig.

After the rare Arch-Poet JOHNSON dy'd,
The Sock grew loathsome, and the Buskins pride,
Together with the Stages glory stood
Each like a poore and pitied widowhood.
The Cirque prophan'd was; and all postures rackt:
For men did strut, and stride, and stare, not act.

Then temper flew from words; and men did squeake,
Looke red, and blow, and bluster, but not speake:
No Holy-Rage, or frantick-fires did stirre,
Or flash about the spacious Theater.   10
No clap of hands, or shout, or praises-proofe
Did crack the Play-house sides, or cleave her roofe.
Artlesse the Sceane was; and that monstrous sin
Of deep and *arrant ignorance* came in;
Such ignorance as theirs was, who once hist
At thy unequal'd Play, the *Alchymist*:
Oh fie upon 'em! Lastly too, all witt
In utter darkenes did, and still will sit
Sleeping the lucklesse Age out, till that she
Her Resurrection ha's again with Thee.   20

To his Nephew, to be prosperous in his art of Painting

On, as thou hast begunne, brave youth, and get
The Palme from *Urbin, Titian, Tintarret,*
Brugel and *Coxie,* and the workes out-doe,
Of *Holben,* and That mighty *Ruben* too.
So draw, and paint, as none may do the like,
No, not the glory of the World, *Vandike.*

Upon Eeles. Epig.

Eeles winds and turnes, and cheats and steales; yet *Eeles*
Driving these sharking trades, is out at heels.

The Dreame

By Dream I saw, one of the three
Sisters of Fate appeare to me:
Close to my Beds side she did stand
Shewing me there a fire brand;
She told me too, as that did spend,

[*The Dreame*] 91

So drew my life unto an end.
Three quarters were consum'd of it;
Onely remaind a little bit,
Which will be burnt up by and by,
Then *Julia* weep, for I must dy.   10

Clothes do but cheat and cousen us

Away with silks, away with Lawn,
Ile have no Sceans, or Curtains drawn:
Give me my Mistresse, as she is,
Drest in her nak't simplicities:
For as my Heart, ene so mine Eye
Is wone with flesh, not *Drapery*.

To Dianeme

Shew me thy feet; shew me thy legs, thy thighes;
Shew me Those *Fleshie Principalities*;
Shew me that Hill (where smiling Love doth sit)
Having a living Fountain under it.
Shew me thy waste; Then let me there withall,
By the *Assention* of thy Lawn, see All.

The mad Maids song

1. Good morrow to the Day so fair;
          Good morning Sir to you:
   Good morrow to mine own torn hair
          Bedabled with the dew.

2. Good morning to this Prim-rose too;
          Good morrow to each maid;
   That will with flowers the *Tomb* bestrew,

                              [*The mad Maids song*]   92

Wherein my Love is laid.

3. Ah woe is me, woe, woe is me,
  Alack and welladay!   10
For pitty, Sir, find out that Bee,
  Which bore my Love away.

4. I'le seek him in your *Bonnet* brave;
  Ile seek him in your eyes;
Nay, now I think th'ave made his grave
  I'th'bed of strawburies.

5. Ile seek him there; I know, ere this,
  The cold, cold Earth doth shake him;
But I will go, or send a kisse
  By you, Sir, to awake him.   20

6. Pray hurt him not; though he be dead,
  He knowes well who do love him,
And who with green-turfes reare his head,
  And who do rudely move him.

7. He's soft and tender (Pray take heed)
  With bands of Cow-slips bind him;
And bring him home, but 'tis decreed,
  That I shall never find him.

Upon Julia's unlacing her self

Tell, if thou canst, (and truly) whence doth come
This *Camphire, Storax, Spiknard, Galbanum:*
These *Musks,* these *Ambers,* and those other smells
(Sweet as the V*estrie of the Oracles.*)
Ile tell thee; while my *Julia* did unlace
Her silken bodies, but a breathing space:
The passive Aire such odour then assum'd,
As when to *Jove* Great *Juno* goes perfum'd.
Whose pure-Immortall body doth transmit
A scent, that fills both Heaven and Earth with it.   10

The Poet loves a Mistresse, but not to marry

1. I do not love to wed,
   Though I do like to wooe;
   And for a maidenhead
   Ile beg, and buy it too.

2. Ile praise, and Ile approve
   Those maids that never vary;
   And fervently Ile love;
   But yet I would not marry.

3. Ile hug, Ile kisse, Ile play,
   And Cock-like Hens Ile tread: 10
   And sport it any way;
   But in the Bridall Bed:

4. For why? that man is poore,
   Who hath but one of many;
   But crown'd he is with store,
   That single may have any.

5. Why then, say, what is he
   (To freedome so unknown)
   Who having two or three,
   Will be content with one?   20

Observation

Who to the North, or South, doth set
His Bed, Male children shall beget.

Putrefaction

Putrefaction is the end
Of all that Nature doth entend.

To Daisies, not to shut so soone

1. Shut not so soon; the dull-ey'd night
        Ha's not as yet begunne
   To make a seisure on the light,
        Or to seale up the Sun.

2. No Marigolds yet closed are;
        No shadowes great appeare;
   Nor doth the early Shepheards Starre
        Shine like a spangle here.

3. Stay but till my *Julia* close
        Her life-begetting eye;   10
   And let the whole world then dispose
        It selfe to live or dye.

Oberons Palace

After the Feast (my *Shapcot*) see,
The Fairie Court I give to thee:
Where we'le present our *Oberon* led
Halfe tipsie to the Fairie Bed,
Where *Mab* he finds; who there doth lie
Not without mickle majesty.
Which, done; and thence remov'd the light,
We'l wish both Them and Thee, good night.

Full as a Bee with Thyme, and Red,
As Cherry harvest, now high fed   10
For Lust and action; on he'l go,
To lye with *Mab*, though all say no.
Lust ha's no eares; He's sharpe as thorn;
And fretfull, carries Hay in's horne,
And lightning in his eyes; and flings
Among the Elves, (if mov'd) the stings
Of peltish wasps; well know his Guard
Kings though th'are hated, will be fear'd.

Wine lead him on. Thus to a Grove
(Sometimes devoted unto Love)   20
Tinseld with *Twilight*, He, and They
Lead by the shine of Snails; a way
Beat with their num'rous feet, which by
Many a neat perplexity,
Many a turn, and man' a crosse-
Track they redeem a bank of mosse
Spungie and swelling, and farre more
Soft then the finest Lemster Ore.
Mildly disparkling, like those fiers,
Which break from the Injeweld tyres   30
Of curious Brides; or like those mites
Of Candi'd dew in Moony nights.
Upon this *Convex*, all the flowers,
(Nature begets by th'Sun, and showers,)
Are to a wilde digestion brought,
As if Loves *Sampler* here was wrought:
Or *Citherea's Ceston*, which
All with temptation doth bewitch.
Sweet Aires move here; and more divine
Made by the breath of great-ey'd kine,   40
Who as they lowe empearl with milk
The four-leav'd grasse, or mosse like silk.
The breath of *Munkies* met to mix
With *Musk-flies*, are th'*Aromaticks*,
Which cense this Arch; and here and there,
And farther off, and every where,
Throughout that *Brave Mosaick* yard
Those Picks or Diamonds in the Card:
With peeps of Harts, of Club and Spade
Are here most neatly inter-laid.   50
Many a Counter, many a Die,
Half rotten, and without an eye,
Lies here abouts; and for to pave
The excellency of this Cave,
Squirrils and childrens teeth late shed,
Are neatly here enchequered
With brownest *Toadstones*, and the Gum
That shines upon the blewer Plum.

The nails faln off by Whit-flawes: Art's
Wise hand enchasing here those warts,   60
Which we to others (from our selves)
Sell, and brought hither by the Elves.
The tempting Mole, stoln from the neck
Of the shie Virgin, seems to deck
The holy Entrance; where within
The roome is hung with the blew skin
Of shifted Snake: enfreez'd throughout
With eyes of Peacocks Trains, & Trout-
flies curious wings; and these among
Those silver-pence, that cut the tongue   70
Of the red infant, neatly hung.
The glow-wormes eyes; the shining scales
Of silv'rie fish; wheat-strawes, the snailes
Soft Candle-light; the Kitling's eyne;
Corrupted wood; serve here for shine.
No glaring light of bold-fac't Day,
Or other over radiant Ray
Ransacks this roome; but ... ak beams
Can make reflected from ... ms,
And multiply; Such is the h...,   80
But ever doubtfull Day, or night.
By this quaint Taper-light he winds
His Errours up; and now he finds
His Moon-tann'd *Mab*, as somewhat sick,
And (Love knowes) tender as a chick.
Upon six plump *Dandillions*, high-
Rear'd, lyes her Elvish-majestie:
Whose woollie-bubbles seem'd to drowne
Her *Mab-ship* in obedient Downe.
For either sheet, was spread the Caule   90
That doth the Infants face enthrall,
When it is born: (by some enstyl'd
The luckie *Omen* of the child)
And next to these two blankets ore-
Cast of finest *Gossamore*.
And then a Rug of carded wooll,
Which, *Spunge-like* drinking in the dull-
Light of the Moon, seem'd to comply,

Cloud-like the *daintie Deitie*.
Thus soft she lies: and over-head   100
A *Spinners* circle is bespread,
With Cob-web-curtains: from the roof
So neatly sunck, as that no proof
Of any tackling can declare
What gives it hanging in the Aire.
The Fringe about this, are those *Threds*
Broke at the Losse of *Maiden-heads:*
And all behung with these pure Pearls,
Dropt from the eyes of *ravisht Girles*
Or *writhing Brides;* when, (panting) they   110
Give unto Love the straiter way.
For Musick now; He has the cries
Of fained-lost-Virginities;
The which the *Elves* make to excite
A more unconquer'd appetite.
The Kings undrest; and now upon
The Gnats-watch-word the *Elves* are gone.
And now the bed, and *Mab* possest
Of this great-little-kingly-Guest.
We'll nobly think, what's to be done,   120
He'll do no doubt; *This flax is spun.*

To Oenone

1. What Conscience, say, is it in thee
          When I a Heart had one,
    To Take away that Heart from me,
          And to retain thy own?

2. For shame or pitty now encline
          To play a loving part;
    Either to send me kindly thine,
          Or give me back my heart.

3. Covet not both; but if thou dost
          Resolve to part with neither;   5

Why! yet to shew that thou art just,
    Take me and mine together.

An Epitaph upon a Virgin

Here a solemne Fast we keepe,
While all beauty lyes asleep
Husht be all things; (no noyse here)
But the toning of a teare:
Or a sigh of such as bring
Cowslips for her covering.

To Jealousie

1. O Jealousie, that art
    The Canker of the heart:
    And mak'st all hell
    Where thou do'st dwell;
    For pitie be
No *Furie,* or no *Fire-brand* to me.

2. Farre from me Ile remove
    All thoughts of irksome Love:
        And turn to snow,
         Or Christall grow;   10
        To keep still free
(O! Soul-tormenting Jealousie,) from Thee.

Upon himself

Come, leave this loathed Country-life, and then
Grow up to be a Roman *Citizen.*
Those mites of Time, which yet remain unspent,
Waste thou in that most Civill Government.

Get their comportment, and the gliding tongue
Of those mild Men, thou art to live among:
Then being seated in that smoother *Sphere,*
Decree thy everlasting *Topick* there.
And to the Farm-house nere return at all;
Though Granges do not love thee, Cities shall.   10

To Blossoms

1. Faire pledges of a fruitfull Tree,
        Why do yee fall so fast?
        Your date is not so past;
    But you may stay yet here a while,
        To blush and gently smile;
            And go at last.

2. What, were yee borne to be
        An houre or half's delight;
        And so to bid goodnight?
    'Twas pitie Nature brought yee forth   10
        Meerly to shew your worth,
            And lose you quite.

3. But you are lovely Leaves, where we
        May read how soon things have
        Their end, though ne'r so brave:
    And after they have shown their pride,
        Like you a while: They glide
            Into the Grave.

Upon his departure hence

Thus I
Passe by,
And die:
As One,

Unknown,
And gon:
I'm made
A shade,
And laid
I'th grave,
There have
My Cave.
Where tell
I dwell,
Farewell.

10

Upon his eye-sight failing him

I beginne to waine in sight;
Shortly I shall bid goodnight:
Then no gazing more about,
When the Tapers once are out.

To a Bed of Tulips

1. Bright Tulips, we do know,
   You had your comming hither;
   And Fading-time do's show,
   That Ye must quickly wither.

2. Your *Sister-hoods* may stay,
   And smile here for your houre;
   But dye ye must away:
   Even as the meanest Flower.

3. Come Virgins then, and see
   Your frailties; and bemone ye;
   For lost like these, 'twill be,
   As Time had never known ye.

10

To the Water Nymphs, drinking at the Fountain

1. Reach, with your whiter hands, to me,
       Some Christall of the Spring;
   And I, about the Cup shall see
       Fresh Lillies flourishing.

2. Or else sweet Nimphs do you but this;
       To'th'Glasse your lips encline;
   And I shall see by that one kisse,
       The Water turn'd to Wine.

Upon a Flie

A Golden Flie one shew'd to me,
Clos'd in a Box of Yvorie:
Where both seem'd proud; the Flie to have
His buriall in an yvory grave:
The yvorie tooke State to hold
A Corps as bright as burnisht gold.
One Fate had both; both equall Grace;
The Buried, and the Burying-place.

Not *Virgils Gnat*, to whom the Spring
All Flowers sent to'is burying.   10
Not *Marshals Bee*, which in a Bead
Of *Amber* quick was buried.
Nor that fine Worme that do's interre
Her selfe i'th'*silken Sepulchre*.
Nor my rare Phil*, that lately was
With Lillies Tomb'd up in a Glasse;
More honour had, then this same *Flie*;
Dead, and clos'd up in *Yvorie*.

   *Sparrow.

To Julia

Julia, when thy *Herrick* dies,
Close thou up thy Poets eyes:
And his last breath, let it be
Taken in by none but Thee.

To the right Honourable Edward Earle of Dorset

If I dare write to You, my Lord, who are,
Of your own selfe, a *Publick Theater.*
And sitting, see the wiles, wayes, walks of wit,
And give a righteous judgement upon it.
What need I care, though some dislike me sho'd,
If *Dorset* say, what *Herrick* writes, is good?
We know y'are learn'd i'th'Muses, and no lesse
In our *State-sanctions,* deep, or bottomlesse.
Whose smile can make a Poet; and your glance
Dash all bad Poems out of countenance.   10

So, that an Author needs no other Bayes
For Coronation, then Your onely Praise.
And no one mischief greater then your frown,
To null his Numbers, and to blast his Crowne.
Few live the life immortall. He ensures
His Fame's long life, who strives to set up Yours.

Upon Love

1. I held Love's head while it did ake;
        But so it chanc't to be;
    The cruell paine did his forsake,
        And forthwith came to me.

2. Ai me! How shal my griefe be stil'd?
        Or where else shall we find
    One like to me, who must be kill'd
        For being too-too-kind?

Come thou, who art the Wine, and wit
      Of all I've writ:
The Grace, the Glorie, and the best
      Piece of the rest.
Thou art of what I did intend
      The All, and End.
And what was made, was made to meet
      Thee, thee my sheet.
Come then, and be to my chast side
      Both Bed, and Bride.   10
We two (as Reliques left) will have
      One Rest, one Grave.
And, hugging close, we will not feare
      Lust entring here:
Where all Desires are dead, or cold
      As is the mould:
And all Affections are forgot,
      Or Trouble not.
Here, here the Slaves and Pris'ners be
      From Shackles free: 20
And weeping Widowes long opprest
      Doe here find rest.
The wronged Client ends his Lawes
      Here, and his Cause.
Here those long suits of Chancery lie
      Quiet, or die:
And all Star-chamber-Bils doe cease,
      Or hold their peace.
Here needs no Court for our Request,
      Where all are best;   30
All wise; all equall; and all just
      Alike i'th'dust.
Nor need we here to feare the frowne
      Of Court, or Crown.
Where Fortune bears no sway o're things,
      There all are Kings.
In this securer place we'l keep,
      As lull'd asleep;

Or for a little time we'l lye,
              As Robes laid by;   40
To be another day re-worne,
              Turn'd, but not torn:
Or like old Testaments ingrost,
              Lockt up, not lost:
And for a while lye here conceal'd,
              To be reveal'd
Next, at that great Platonick yeere,
              And then meet here.

To Phillis to love, and live with him

Live, live with me, and thou shalt see
The pleasures Ile prepare for thee:
What sweets the Country can afford
Shall blesse thy Bed, and blesse thy Board.
The soft sweet Mosse shall be thy bed,
With crawling Woodbine over-spread:
By which the silver-shedding streames
Shall gently melt thee into dreames.
Thy clothing next, shall be a Gowne
Made of the Fleeces purest Downe.   10
The tongues of Kids shall be thy meate;
Their Milke thy drinke; and thou shalt eate
The Paste of Filberts for thy bread
With Cream of Cowslips buttered:
Thy Feasting-Tables shall be Hills
With *Daisies* spread, and *Daffadils;*
Where thou shalt sit, and *Red-brest* by,
For meat, shall give thee melody.
Ile give thee Chaines and Carkanets
Of *Primroses* and *Violets.*   20
A Bag and Bottle thou shalt have;
That richly wrought, and This as brave;
So that as either shall expresse
The Wearer's no meane Shepheardesse.
At Sheering-times, and yearely Wakes,
When *Themilis* his pastime makes,

There thou shalt be; and be the wit,
Nay more, the Feast, and grace of it.
On Holy-dayes, when Virgins meet
To dance the Heyes with nimble feet;   30
Thou shalt come forth, and then appeare
The *Queen of Roses* for that yeere.
And having danc't ('bove all the best)
Carry the Garland from the rest.
In Wicker-baskets Maids shal bring
To thee, (my dearest Shephardling)
The blushing Apple, bashfull Peare,
And shame-fac't Plum, (all simp'ring there).
Walk in the Groves, and thou shalt find
The name of *Phillis* in the Rind   40
Of every straight, and smooth-skin tree;
Where kissing that, Ile twice kisse thee.
To thee a Sheep-hook I will send,
Be-pranckt with Ribbands, to this end,
This, this alluring Hook might be
Lesse for to catch a sheep, then me.
Thou shalt have Possets, Wassails fine,
Not made of Ale, but spiced Wine;
To make thy Maids and selfe free mirth,
All sitting neer the glitt'ring Hearth.   50
Thou sha't have Ribbands, Roses, Rings,'
Gloves, Garters, Stockings, Shooes, and Strings
Of winning Colours, that shall move
Others to Lust, but me to Love.
These (nay) and more, thine own shal be,
If thou wilt love, and live with me.

Upon her feet

     Her pretty feet
       Like snailes did creep
   A little out, and then,
As if they started at Bo-peep,
   Did soon draw in agen.

Ill Government

Preposterous is that Government, (and rude)
When Kings obey the wilder Multitude.

Anacreontike

Born I was to be old,
    And for to die here:
After that, in the mould
    Long for to lye here.
But before that day comes,
    Still I be Bousing;
For I know, in the Tombs
    There's no Carousing.

An Ode to Sir Clipsebie Crew

1. Here we securely live, and eate
        The Creame of meat;
    And keep eternal fires,
By which we sit, and doe Divine
        As Wine
    And Rage inspires.

2. If full we charme; then call upon
    Anacreon
    To grace the frantick Thyrse:
And having drunk, we raise a shout   10
        Throughout
    To praise his Verse.

3. Then cause we *Horace* to be read,
        Which sung, or seyd,
    A Goblet, to the brim,

Of Lyrick Wine, both swell'd and crown'd,
    A Round
      We quaffe to him.

4. Thus, thus, we live, and spend the houres
    In Wine and Flowers: 20
  And make the frollick yeere,
The Month, the Week, the instant Day
      To stay
    The longer here.

5. Come then, brave Knight, and see the Cell
    Wherein I dwell;
  And my Enchantments too;
Which Love and noble freedome is;
      And this
    Shall fetter you.   30

6. Take Horse, and come; or be so kind,
    To send your mind
  (Though but in Numbers few)
And I shall think I have the heart,
      Or part
    Of *Clipseby Crew*.

To his Tomb-maker

Go I must; when I am gone,
Write but this upon my Stone;
Chaste I liv'd, without a wife,
That's the Story of my life.
Strewings need none, every flower
Is in this word, Batchelour.

His content in the Country

Here, here I live with what my Board,
Can with the smallest cost afford.

Though ne'r so mean the Viands be,
They well content my *Prew* and me.
Or Pea, or Bean, or Wort, or Beet,
What ever comes, content makes sweet:
Here we rejoyce, because no Rent
We pay for our poore Tenement:
Wherein we rest, and never feare
The Landlord, or the Usurer.   10
The Quarter-day do's ne'r affright
Our peacefull slumbers in the night.
We eate our own, and batten more,
Because we feed on no mans score:
But pitie those, whose flanks grow great,
Swel'd with the Lard of others meat.
We blesse our Fortunes, when we see
Our own beloved privacie:
And like our living, where w'are known
To very few, or else to none.   20

Art above Nature, to Julia

When I behold a Forrest spread
With silken trees upon thy head;
And when I see that other Dresse
Of flowers set in comlinesse:
When I behold another grace
In the ascent of curious Lace,
Which like a Pinacle doth shew
The top, and the top-gallant too.
Then, when I see thy Tresses bound
Into an Ovall, square, or round;   10
And knit in knots far more then I
Can tell by tongue; or true-love tie:
Next, when those Lawnie Filmes I see
Play with a wild civility:
And all those airie silks to flow,
Alluring me, and tempting so:
I must confesse, mine eye and heart
Dotes less on Nature, then on Art.

Upon the losse of his Finger

One of the five straight branches of my hand
Is lopt already; and the rest but stand
Expecting when to fall: which soon will be;
First dyes the Leafe, the Bough next, next the Tree.

Upon Irene

Angry if *Irene* be
But a Minutes life with me:
Such a fire I espie
Walking in and out her eye,
As at once I freeze, and frie.

The Apparition of his Mistresse
calling him to Elizium

     Desunt nonnulla————

Come then, and like two Doves with silv'rie wings,
Let our soules flie to'th'shades, where ever springs
Sit smiling in the Meads; where Balme and Oile,
Roses and Cassia crown the untill'd soyle.
Where no disease raignes, or infection comes
To blast the Aire, but *Amber-greece* and *Gums*.
This, that, and ev'ry Thicket doth transpire
More sweet, then *Storax* from the hallowed fire:
Where ev'ry tree a wealthy issue beares   10
Of fragrant Apples, blushing Plums, or Peares:
And all the shrubs, with sparkling spangles, shew
Like Morning-Sun-shine tinsilling the dew.
Here in green Meddowes sits eternall May,
Purfling the Margents, while perpetuall Day
So double gilds the Aire, as that no night
Can ever rust th'Enamel of the light.
Here, naked Younglings, handsome Striplings run
Their Goales for Virgins kisses; which when done,

Then unto Dancing forth the learned Round   20
Commixt they meet, with endlesse Roses crown'd.
And here we'l sit on Primrose-banks, and see
Love's *Chorus* led by *Cupid;* and we'l be
Two loving followers too unto the Grove,
Where Poets sing the stories of our love.
There thou shalt hear Divine *Musæus* sing
Of *Hero*, and *Leander;* then Ile bring
Thee to the Stand, where honour'd *Homer* reades
His *Odisees*, and his high *Iliades*.
About whose Throne the crowd of Poets throng   30
To heare the incantation of his tongue:
To *Linus*, then to *Pindar;* and that done,
Ile bring thee *Herrick* to *Anacreon*,
Quaffing his full-crown'd bowles of burning Wine,
And in his Raptures speaking Lines of Thine,
Like to His subject; and as his Frantick-
Looks, shew him truly *Bacchanalian* like,
Besmear'd with Grapes; welcome he shall thee thither,
Where both may rage, both drink and dance together.
Then stately *Virgil*, witty *Ovid*, by   40
Whom faire *Corinna* sits, and doth comply
With Yvorie wrists, his Laureat head, and steeps
His eye in dew of kisses, while he sleeps.
Then soft *Catullus*, sharp-fang'd *Martial*,
And towring *Lucan, Horace, Juvenal*,
And Snakie *Perseus*, these, and those, whom Rage
(Dropt from the jarres of heaven) fill'd t'engage
All times unto their frenzies; Thou shalt there
Behold them in a spacious Theater.
Among which glories, (crown'd with sacred Bayes,   50
And flatt'ring Ivie) Two recite their Plaies,
Beumont and *Fletcher*, Swans, to whom all eares
Listen, while they (like Syrens in their Spheres)
Sing their *Evadne;* and still more for thee
There yet remaines to know, then thou can'st see
By glim'ring of a fancie: Doe but come,
And there Ile shew thee that capacious roome
In which thy Father *Johnson* now is plac't,
As in a Globe of Radiant fire, and grac't

To be in that Orbe crown'd (that doth include   60
Those Prophets of the former Magnitude)
And be our chiefe; But harke, I heare the Cock,
(The Bell-man of the night) proclaime the clock
Of late struck one; and now I see the prime
Of Day break from the pregnant East, 'tis time
I vanish; more I had to say;
But Night determines here, Away.

The Primrose

1. Aske me why I send you here
This sweet *Infanta* of the yeere?
   Aske me why I send to you
This Primrose, thus bepearl'd with dew?
   I will whisper to your eares,
The sweets of Love are mixt with tears.

2. Ask me why this flower do's show
So yellow-green, and sickly too?
   Ask me why the stalk is weak
And bending, (yet it doth not break?)   10
   I will answer, These discover
What fainting hopes are in a Lover.

No luck in Love

1. I doe love I know not what;
   Sometimes this, & sometimes that:
   All conditions I aime at.

2. But, as lucklesse, I have yet
   Many shrewd disasters met,
   To gaine her whom I wo'd get.

3. Therefore now Ile love no more,
   As I've doted heretofore:
   He who must be, shall be poore.

A charme, or an allay for Love

If so be a Toad be laid
In a Sheeps-skin newly flaid,
And that ty'd to man 'twil sever
Him and his affections ever.

The Head-ake

1. My head doth ake,
O *Sappho!* take
   Thy fillit,
And bind the paine;
Or bring some bane
   To kill it.

2. But lesse that part,
Then my poore heart,
   Now is sick:
One kisse from thee
Will counsell be,
   And Physick.

To his Booke

Be bold my Booke, nor be abasht, or feare
The cutting Thumb-naile, or the Brow severe.
But by the *Muses* sweare, all here is good,
If but well read; or ill read, understood .

His Prayer to Ben. Johnson

1. When I a Verse shall make,
   Know I have praid thee,
   For old *Religions* sake,
   Saint *Ben* to aide me.

2. Make the way smooth for me,
   When I, thy *Herrick,*
   Honouring thee, on my knee
   Offer my *Lyrick.*

3. Candles Ile give to thee,
   And a new Altar;   10
   And thou Saint *Ben,* shalt be
   Writ in my *Psalter.*

The bad season makes the Poet sad

Dull to my selfe, and almost dead to these
My many fresh and fragrant Mistresses:
Lost to all Musick now; since every thing
Puts on the semblance here of sorrowing.
Sick is the Land to'th'heart; and doth endure
More dangerous faintings by her desp'rate cure.
But if that golden Age wo'd come again,
And *Charles* here Rule, as he before did Raign;
If smooth and unperplext the Seasons were,
As when the *Sweet Maria* lived here: 10
I sho'd delight to have my Curles halfe drown'd
In *Tyrian Dewes,* and Head with Roses crown'd.
And once more yet (ere I am laid out dead)
Knock at a Starre with my exalted Head.

The Night-piece, to Julia

1. Her Eyes the Glow-worme lend thee,
   The Shooting Starres attend thee;
         And the Elves also,
         Whose little eyes glow,
   Like the sparks of fire, befriend thee.

2. No *Will-o'th'-Wispe* mis-light thee;
   Nor Snake, or Slow-worme bite thee:
         But on, on thy way

>   Not making a stay,
> Since Ghost ther's none to affright thee.   10

3. Let not the darke thee cumber;
    What though the Moon do's slumber?
        The Starres of the night
        Will lend thee their light,
Like Tapers cleare without number.

4. Then *Julia* let me wooe thee,
    Thus, thus to come unto me:
        And when I shall meet
        Thy silv'ry feet,
My soule Ile poure into thee.   20

Glorie

I make no haste to have my Numbers read.
Seldome comes Glorie till a man be dead.

Poets

Wantons we are; and though our words be such,
Our Lives do differ from our Lines by much.

No despight to the dead

Reproach we may the living; not the dead:
'Tis cowardice to bite the buried.

The Coblers Catch

Come sit we by the fires side;
   And roundly drinke we here;
Till that we see our cheekes Ale-dy'd
   And noses tann'd with Beere.

The Beggar to Mab, the Fairie Queen

Please your Grace, from out your Store,
Give an Almes to one that's poore,
That your mickle, may have more.
Black I'm grown for want of meat;
Give me then an Ant to eate;
Or the cleft eare of a Mouse
Over-sowr'd in drinke of Souce:
Or *sweet Lady* reach to me
The *Abdomen* of a Bee;
Or commend a *Crickets-hip*,   10
Or his *Huckson,* to my Scrip.
Give for bread, a little bit
Of a Pease, that 'gins to chit,
And my full thanks take for it.
Floure of Fuz-balls, that's too good
For a man in needy-hood:
But the Meal of Mill-dust can
Well content a craving man.
Any Orts the Elves refuse
Well will serve the Beggars use.   20
But if this may seem too much
For an Almes; then give me such
Little bits, that nestle there
In the Pris'ners *Panier.*
So a blessing light upon
You, and mighty *Oberon:*
That your plenty last till when,
I return your Almes agen.

The Hag

1. The Hag is astride,
    This night for to ride;
The Devill and shee together:
    Through thick, and through thin,
    Now out, and then in,
Though ne'r so foule be the weather.

2. A Thorn or a Burr
   She takes for a Spurre:
With a lash of a Bramble she rides now,
   Through Brakes and through Bryars,   10
   O're Ditches, and Mires,
She followes the Spirit that guides now.

3. No Beast, for his food,
   Dares now range the wood;
But husht in his laire he lies lurking:
   While mischeifs, by these,
   On Land and on Seas,
At noone of Night are a working.

4. The storme will arise,
   And trouble the skies;   20
This night, and more for the wonder,
   The ghost from the Tomb
   Affrighted shall come,
Cal'd out by the clap of the Thunder.

The Country Life

TO THE HONOURED M. END. PORTER,
GROOME OF THE BED-CHAMBER TO HIS MAJ.

Sweet Country life, to such unknown,
Whose lives are others, not their own!
But serving Courts, and Cities, be
Less happy, less enjoying thee.
Thou never Plow'st the Oceans foame
To seek, and bring rough Pepper home:
Nor to the Eastern Ind dost rove
To bring from thence the scorched Clove.
Nor, with the losse of thy lov'd rest,
Bring'st home the Ingot from the West.   10
No, thy Ambition's Master-piece
Flies no thought higher then a fleece:

Or how to pay thy Hinds, and cleere
All scores; and so to end the yeere:
But walk'st about thine own dear bounds,
Not envying others larger grounds:
For well thou know'st, *'tis not th'extent*
Of Land makes life, but sweet content.
When now the Cock (the Plow-mans Horne)
Calls forth the lilly-wristed Morne;   20
Then to thy corn-fields thou dost goe,
Which though well soyl'd, yet thou dost know,
That the best compost for the Lands
Is the wise Masters Feet, and Hands.
There at the Plough thou find'st thy Teame,
With a Hind whistling there to them:
And cheer'st them up, by singing how
The Kingdoms portion *is the Plow*.
This done, then to th'enameld Meads
Thou go'st; and as thy foot there treads,   30
Thou seest a present God-like Power
Imprinted in each Herbe and Flower:
And smell'st the breath of great-ey'd Kine,
Sweet as the blossomes of the Vine.
Here thou behold'st thy large sleek Neat
Unto the Dew-laps up in meat:
And, as thou look'st, the wanton Steere,
The Heifer, Cow, and Oxe draw neere
To make a pleasing pastime there.
These seen, thou go'st to view thy flocks   40
Of sheep, (safe from the Wolfe and Fox)
And find'st their bellies there as full
Of short sweet grasse, as backs with wool.
And leav'st them (as they feed and fill)
A Shepherd piping on a hill.
For Sports, for Pagentrie, and Playes,
Thou hast thy Eves, and Holydayes:
On which the young men and maids meet,
To exercise their dancing feet:
Tripping the comely country round,   50
With Daffadils and Daisies crown'd.

[*The Country Life*] 118

Thy Wakes, thy Quintels, here thou hast,
Thy May-poles too with Garlands grac't:
Thy Morris-dance; thy Whitsun-ale;
Thy Sheering-feast, which never faile.
Thy Harvest home; thy Wassaile bowle,
That's tost up after Fox i'th'Hole.
Thy Mummeries; thy Twelfe-tide Kings
And Queenes; thy Christmas revellings:
Thy Nut-browne mirth; thy Russet wit;   60
And no man payes too deare for it.
To these, thou hast thy times to goe
And trace the Hare i'th'trecherous Snow:
Thy witty wiles to draw, and get
The Larke into the Trammell net:
Thou hast thy Cockrood, and thy Glade
To take the precious Phesant made:
Thy Lime-twigs, Snares, and Pit-falls then
To catch the pilfring Birds, not Men.
O happy life! if that their good   70
The Husbandmen but understood!
Who all the day themselves doe please,
And Younglings, with such sports as these.
And, lying down, have nought t'affright
Sweet sleep, that makes more short the night.
> *Cætera desunt*————

To Electra

1. I dare not ask a kisse;
   I dare not beg a smile;
Lest having that, or this,
   I might grow proud the while.

2. No, no, the utmost share
   Of my desire, shall be
Onely to kisse that Aire,
   That lately kissed thee.

To Fortune

Tumble me down, and I will sit
Upon my ruines (smiling yet:)
Teare me to tatters; yet I'le be
Patient in my necessitie.
Laugh at my scraps of cloaths, and shun
Me, as a fear'd infection:
Yet scarre-crow-like I'le walk, as one,
Neglecting thy derision.

Upon his Verses

What off-spring other men have got,
The how, where, when, I question not.
These are the Children I have left;
Adopted some; none got by theft.
But all are toucht (like lawfull plate)
And no Verse illegitimate.

The Funerall Rites of the Rose

The Rose was sick, and smiling di'd;
And (being to be sanctifi'd)
About the Bed, there sighing stood
The sweet, and flowrie Sisterhood.
Some hung the head, while some did bring
(To wash her) water from the Spring.
Some laid her forth, while other wept,
But all a solemne Fast there kept.
The holy Sisters some among
The sacred *Dirge* and *Trentall* sung.   10
But ah! what sweets smelt every where,
As Heaven had spent all perfumes there.
At last, when prayers for the dead,

And Rites were all accomplished;
They, weeping, spread a Lawnie Loome,
And clos'd her up, as in a Tombe.

The May-pole

The May-pole is up,
Now give me the cup;
I'le drink to the Garlands a-round it:
But first unto those
Whose hands did compose
The glory of flowers that crown'd it.

A health to my Girles,
Whose husbands may Earles
Or Lords be, (granting my wishes)
And when that ye wed   10
To the Bridall Bed,
Then multiply all, like to Fishes.

Men mind no state in sicknesse

That flow of Gallants which approach
To kisse thy hand from out the coach;
That fleet of Lackeyes, which do run
Before thy swift Postilion;
Those strong-hoof'd Mules, which we behold,
Rein'd in with Purple, Pearl, and gold,
And shod with silver, prove to be
The drawers of the *axeltree*.
Thy Wife, thy Children, and the state
Of *Persian* Loomes, and *antique* Plate: 10
All these, and more, shall then afford
No joy to thee their sickly Lord.

The Bracelet of Pearle: to Silvia

I brake thy Bracelet 'gainst my will;
   And, wretched, I did see
Thee discomposed then, and still
   Art discontent with me.

One jemme was lost; and I will get
   A richer pearle for thee,
Then ever, dearest *Silvia*, yet
   Was drunk to *Antonie*.

Or, for revenge, I'le tell thee what
   Thou for the breach shalt do;   10
First, crack the strings, and after that,
   Cleave thou my heart in two.

His returne to London

From the dull confines of the drooping West,
To see the day spring from the pregnant East,
Ravisht in spirit, I come, nay more, I flie
To thee, blest place of my Nativitie!
Thus, thus with hallowed foot I touch the ground,
With thousand blessings by thy Fortune crown'd.
O fruitfull Genius! that bestowest here
An everlasting plenty, yeere by yeere.
O Place! O People! Manners! fram'd to please
All *Nations, Customes, Kindreds, Languages!*   10
I am a free-born *Roman;* suffer then,
That I amongst you live a Citizen.
London my home is: though by hard fate sent
Into a long and irksome banishment;
Yet since cal'd back; henceforward let me be,
O native countrey, repossest by thee!
For, rather then I'le to the West return,
I'le beg of thee first here to have mine Urn.

Weak I am grown, and must in short time fall;
Give thou my sacred Reliques Buriall.   20

Not every day fit for Verse

'Tis not ev'ry day, that I
Fitted am to prophesie:
No, but when the Spirit fils
The fantastick Pannicles:
Full of fier; then I write
As the Godhead doth indite.
Thus inrag'd, my lines are hurl'd,
Like the *Sybells*, through the world.
Look how next the holy fier
Either slakes, or doth retire;   10
So the Fancie cooles, till when
That brave Spirit comes agen.

Proof to no purpose

You see this gentle streame, that glides,
Shov'd on, by quick succeeding Tides:
Trie if this sober streame you can
Follow to th'wilder Ocean:
And see, if there it keeps unspent
In that congesting element.
Next, from that world of waters, then
By poares and cavernes back agen
Induc't that inadultrate same
Streame to the Spring from whence it came.   10
This with a wonder when ye do,
As easie, and els easier too:
Then may ye recollect the graines
Of my particular Remaines;
After a thousand Lusters hurld,
By ruffling winds, about the world.

   Though Clock,
To tell how night drawes hence, I've none,
   A Cock,
I have, to sing how day drawes on.
   I have
A maid (my *Prew*) by good luck sent,
   To save
That little, Fates me gave or lent.
   A Hen
I keep, which creeking day by day,   10
   Tells when
She goes her long white egg to lay.
   A goose
I have, which, with a jealous eare,
   Lets loose
Her tongue, to tell what danger's neare.
   A Lamb
I keep (tame) with my morsells fed,
   Whose Dam
An Orphan left him (lately dead.)   20
   A Cat
I keep, that playes about my House,
   Grown fat,
With eating many a miching Mouse.
   To these
A *Trasy** I do keep, whereby
   I please
The more my rurall privacie:
   Which are
But toyes, to give my heart some ease: 30
   Where care
None is, slight things do lightly please.

 *His Spaniel.

       Begin with a kisse,
       Go on too with this:
And thus, thus, thus let us smother
       Our lips for a while,
       But let's not beguile
Our hope of one for the other.

       This play, be assur'd,
       Long enough has endur'd,
Since more and more is exacted;
       For love he doth call   10
       For his Uptailes all;
And that's the part to be acted.

A Ternarie of littles,
upon a pipkin of Jellie sent to a Lady

1 A little Saint best fits a little Shrine,
   A little prop best fits a little Vine,
   As my small Cruse best fits my little Wine.

2 A little Seed best fits a little Soyle,
   A little Trade best fits a little Toyle:
   As my small Jarre best fits my little Oyle.

3 A little Bin best fits a little Bread,
   A little Garland fits a little Head:
   As my small stuffe best fits my little Shed.

4 A little Hearth best fits a little Fire,   10
   A little Chappell fits a little Quire,
   As my small Bell best fits my little Spire.

5 A little streame best fits a little Boat;
   A little lead best fits a little Float;
   As my small Pipe best fits my little note.

6 A little meat best fits a little bellie,
  As sweetly Lady, give me leave to tell ye,
  This little Pipkin fits this little Jellie.

The Smell of the Sacrifice

The Gods require the thighes
Of Beeves for sacrifice;
Which rosted, we the steam
Must sacrifice to them:
Who though they do not eat,
Yet love the smell of meat.

Lovers how they come and part

A gyges Ring they beare about them still,
To be, and not seen when and where they will.
They tread on clouds, and though they sometimes fall,
They fall like dew, but make no noise at all.
So silently they one to th'other come,
As colours steale into the Peare or Plum,
And Aire-like, leave no pression to be seen
Where e're they met, or parting place has been.

The Wake

Come *Anthea* let us two
Go to Feast, as others do.
Tarts and Custards, Creams and Cakes,
Are the Junketts still at Wakes:
Unto which the Tribes resort,

Where the businesse is the sport:
Morris-dancers thou shalt see,
Marian too in Pagentrie:
And a Mimick to devise
Many grinning properties.   10
Players there will be, and those
Base in action as in clothes:
Yet with strutting they will please
The incurious Villages.
Neer the dying of the day,
There will be a *Cudgell*-Play,
Where a *Coxcomb* will be broke,
Ere a good *word* can be spoke:
But the anger ends all here,
Drencht in Ale, or drown'd in Beere.   20
Happy Rusticks, best content
With the cheapest Merriment:
And possesse no other feare,
Then to want the Wake next Yeare.

A Conjuration, to Electra

By those soft Tods of wooll
With which the aire is full:
By all those Tinctures there,
That paint the *Hemisphere*:
By Dewes and drisling Raine,
That swell the Golden Graine:
By all those sweets that be
I'th flowrie Nunnerie:
By silent Nights, and the
Three Formes of Heccate: 10
By all Aspects that blesse
The sober Sorceresse,
While juice she straines, and pith
To make her Philters with:
By Time, that hastens on

Things to perfection:
And by your self, the best
Conjurement of the rest:
O my *Electra!* be
In love with none, but me.

A Hymne to Bacchus

I sing thy praise *Iacchus*,
Who with thy *Thyrse* dost thwack us:
And yet thou so dost back us
With boldness that we feare
No *Brutus* entring here;
Nor *Cato* the severe.
What though the *Lictors* threat us,
We know they dare not beate us;
So long as thou dost heat us.
When we thy *Orgies* sing,   10
Each Cobler is a King;
Nor dreads he any thing:
And though he doe not rave,
Yet he'l the courage have
To call my *Lord Maior* knave;
Besides too, in a brave,
Although he has no riches,
But walks with dangling breeches,
And skirts that want their stiches,
And shewes his naked flitches;   20
Yet he'le be thought or seen,
So good as *George-a-Green*;
And calls his Blouze, his Queene;
And speaks in language keene:
O *Bacchus!* let us be
From cares and troubles free;
And thou shalt heare how we
Will chant new *Hymnes* to thee.

When as in silks my *Julia* goes,
Then, then (me thinks) how sweetly flowes
That liquefaction of her clothes.

Next, when I cast mine eyes and see
That brave Vibration each way free;
O how that glittering taketh me!

Upon Prew his Maid

In this little Urne is laid
Prewdence Baldwin (once my maid)
From whose happy spark here let
Spring the purple Violet.

The Amber Bead

I saw a Flie within a Beade
Of Amber cleanly buried:
The Urne was little, but the room
More rich then *Cleopatra's* Tombe.

The Transfiguration

Immortall clothing I put on,
So soone as *Julia* I am gon
To mine eternall Mansion.

Thou, thou art here, to humane sight
Cloth'd all with incorrupted light;
But yet how more admir'dly bright

Wilt thou appear, when thou art set
In thy refulgent Thronelet,
That shin'st thus in thy counterfeit?

Upon Love

Love is a Circle, and an Endlesse Sphere;
From good to good, revolving here, & there.

No difference i'th'dark

Night makes no difference 'twixt the Priest and Clark;
Jone as my Lady is as good i'th'dark.

The Body

The Body is the Soules poore house, or home,
Whose Ribs the Laths are, & whose Flesh the Loame.

Kisses Loathsome

I abhor the slimie kisse,
(Which to me most loathsome is.)
Those lips please me which are plac't
Close, but not too strictly lac't:
Yielding I wo'd have them; yet
Not a wimbling Tongue admit:
What sho'd poking-sticks make there,
When the ruffe is set elsewhere?

Charmes

Bring the holy crust of Bread,
Lay it underneath the head;
'Tis a certain Charm to keep
Hags away, while Children sleep.

The Ceremonies for Candlemasse day

Kindle the Christmas Brand, and then
    Till Sunne-set, let it burne;
Which quencht, then lay it up agen,
    Till Christmas next returne.

Part must be kept wherewith to teend
    The Christmas Log next yeare;
And where 'tis safely kept, the Fiend,
    Can do no mischiefe (there.)

Upon Ben. Johnson

Here lyes *Johnson* with the rest
Of the Poets; but the Best.
Reader, wo'dst thou more have known?
Aske his Story, not this Stone.
That will speake what this can't tell
Of his glory. *So farewell.*

An Ode for him

    Ah *Ben!*
    Say how, or when
    Shall we thy Guests
    Meet at those *Lyrick* Feasts,

Made at the *Sun,*
The *Dog,* the triple *Tunne?*
Where we such clusters had,
As made us nobly wild, not mad;
And yet each Verse of thine
Out-did the meate, out-did the frolick wine.　　　10

My *Ben*
Or come agen:
Or send to us,
Thy wits great over-plus;
But teach us yet
Wisely to husband it;
Lest we that Tallent spend:
And having once brought to an end
That precious stock; the store
Of such a wit the world sho'd have no more.　　　20

The present time best pleaseth

Praise they that will Times past, I joy to see
My selfe now live: *this age best pleaseth mee.*

Cloathes, are conspirators

Though from without no foes at all we feare;
We shall be wounded by the cloathes we weare.

Upon Julia's washing her self in the river

How fierce was I, when I did see
My *Julia* wash her self in thee!
So *Lillies* thorough Christall look:

[*Upon Julie's washing her self in the river*]　　132

So purest pebbles in the brook:
As in the River *Julia* did,
Halfe with a Lawne of water hid,
Into thy streames my self I threw,
And strugling there, I kist thee too;
And more had done (it is confest)
Had not thy waves forbad the rest.   10

Upon Blisse

Blisse (last night drunk) did kisse his mothers knee:
Where he will kisse (next drunk) conjecture ye.

On Himselfe

Lost to the world; lost to my selfe; alone
Here now I rest under this Marble stone:
In depth of silence, heard, and seene of none.

Anacreontike

    I must
    Not trust
Here to any;
    Bereav'd,
    Deceiv'd
By so many;
    As one
    Undone
By my losses;
    Comply   10
    Will I
With my crosses.

```
            Yet still
            I will
Not be grieving;
            Since thence
            And hence
Comes relieving.
            But this
            Sweet is                                    20
In our mourning;
            Times bad
            And sad
Are a turning:
            And he
            Whom we
See dejected;
            Next day
            Wee may
See erected.                                            30
```

Anacrontick Verse

Brisk methinks I am, and fine,
When I drinke my capring wine:
Then to love I do encline;
When I drinke my wanton wine:
And I wish all maidens mine,
When I drinke my sprightly wine:
Well I sup, and well I dine,
When I drinke my frolick wine:
But I languish, lowre, and Pine,
When I want my fragrant wine.   10

Parcell-gil't-Poetry

Let's strive to be the best; the Gods, we know it,
Pillars and men, hate an indifferent Poet.

Upon Love, by way of question and answer

I bring ye love, *Quest*. What will love do?
    Ans. Like, and dislike ye:
I bring ye love: *Quest*. What will love do?
    Ans. Stroake ye to strike ye.
I bring ye love: *Quest*. What will love do?
    Ans. Love will be-foole ye:
I bring ye love: *Quest*. What will love do?
    Ans. Heate ye to coole ye:
I bring ye love: *Quest*. What will love do?
    Ans. Love gifts will send ye: 10
I bring ye love: *Quest*. What will love do?
    Ans. Stock ye to spend ye:
I bring ye love: *Quest*. What will love do?
    Ans. Love will fulfill ye:
I bring ye love: *Quest*. What will love do?
    Ans. Kisse ye, to kill ye.

The Vision

Me thought I saw (as I did dreame in bed)
A crawling Vine about *Anacreon*'s head:
Flusht was his face; his haires with oyle did shine;
And as he spake, his mouth ranne ore with wine.
Tipled he was; and tipling lispt withall;
And lisping reeld, and reeling like to fall.
A young *Enchantresse* close by him did stand
Tapping his plump thighes with a *mirtle* wand:
She smil'd; he kist; and kissing, cull'd her too;
And being cup-shot, more he co'd not doe.   10
For which (me thought) in prittie anger she
Snatch off his Crown, and gave the wreath to me:
Since when (me thinks) my braines about doe swim,
And I am wilde and wanton like to him.

Comfort to a youth that had lost his Love

What needs complaints,
    When she a place
Has with the race
    Of Saints?
In endlesse mirth,
She thinks not on
What's said or done
    In earth:
She sees no teares,
Or any tone   10
Of thy deep grone
    She heares:
Nor do's she minde,
Or think on't now,
That ever thou
    Wast kind.
But chang'd above,
She likes not there,
As she did here,
    Thy Love.   20
Forbeare therefore,
And Lull asleepe
Thy woes and weep
    No more.

Peace not Permanent

Great Cities seldome rest: If there be none
T'invade from far: They'l finde worse foes at home.

His desire

Give me a man that is not dull,
When all the world with rifts is full:

But unamaz'd dares clearely sing,
When as the roof's a tottering:
And, though it falls, continues still
Tickling the *Citterne* with his quill.

The Tinkers Song

Along, come along,
Let's meet in a throng
      Here of Tinkers;
And quaffe up a Bowle
As big as a Cowle
      To Beer Drinkers.
The pole of the Hop
Place in the Ale-shop
      to Bethwack us;
If ever we think   10
So much as to drink
      Unto *Bacchus*.
Who frolick will be,
For little cost he
      Must not vary,
From Beer-broth at all,
So much as to call
      For Canary.

Another on Love

Love's of it self, too sweet; the best of all
Is, when loves hony has a dash of gall.

To his Girles who would have him sportfull

Alas I can't, for tell me how
Can I be gamesome (aged now)

[*To his Girles who would have him sportfull*]   137

Besides ye see me daily grow
Here Winter-like, to Frost and Snow.
And I ere long, my Girles, shall see,
Ye quake for cold to looke on me.

On himselfe

One Eare tingles; some there be,
That are snarling now at me:
Be they those that *Homer* bit,
I will give them thanks for it.

Upon Spur

Spur jingles now, and sweares by no meane oathes,
He's double honour'd, since h'as got gay cloathes:
Most like his Suite, and all commend the Trim;
And thus they praise the Sumpter; but not him:
As to the Goddesse, people did conferre
Worship, and not to'th'Asse that carried her.

The Hagg

The staffe is now greas'd,
And very well pleas'd,
She cockes out her Arse at the parting,
To an old Ram Goat,
That rattles i'th'throat,
Halfe choakt with the stink of her farting.

In a dirtie Haire-lace

She leads on a brace
Of black-bore-cats to attend her;
Who scratch at the Moone,   10
And threaten at noone
Of night from Heaven for to rend her.

A hunting she goes;
A crackt horne she blowes;
At which the hounds fall a bounding;
While th'Moone in her sphere
Peepes trembling for feare,
And night's afraid of the sounding.

To his Booke

Goe thou forth my booke, though late;
Yet be timely fortunate.
It may chance good-luck may send
Thee a kinsman, or a friend,
That may harbour thee, when I,
With my fates neglected lye.
If thou know'st not where to dwell,
See, the fier's by: *Farewell.*

On Himselfe

The worke is done: young men, and maidens set
Upon my curles the *Mirtle Coronet,*
Washt with sweet ointments; Thus at last I come
To suffer in the Muses *Martyrdome:*
But with this comfort, if my blood be shed,
The Muses will weare blackes, when I am dead.

Fames pillar here, at last, we set,
Out-during *Marble, Brasse,* or *Jet,*
    Charm'd and enchanted so,
    As to withstand the blow
        Of   overthrow:
        Nor shall the seas,
        Or   OUTRAGES
        Of storms orebear
        What we up-rear,
        Tho Kingdoms fal,
    This pillar never shall
    Decline or waste at all;
But stand for ever by his owne.
Firme and well fixt foundation.

To his Book's end this last line he'd have plac't,
Jocond his Muse was; but his Life was chast.

His Letanie, to the Holy Spirit

1. In the houre of my distresse,
   When temptations me oppresse,
   And when I my sins confesse,
   	Sweet Spirit comfort me!

2. When I lie within my bed,
   Sick in heart, and sick in head,
   And with doubts discomforted,
   	Sweet Spirit comfort me!

3. When the house doth sigh and weep,
   And the world is drown'd in sleep,	10
   Yet mine eyes the watch do keep;
   	Sweet Spirit comfort me!

4. When the artlesse Doctor sees
   No one hope, but of his Fees,
   And his skill runs on the lees;
   	Sweet Spirit comfort me!

5. When his Potion and his Pill,
   His, or none, or little skill,
   Meet for nothing, but to kill;
   	Sweet Spirit comfort me!	20

6. When the passing-bell doth tole,
   And the Furies in a shole
   Come to fright a parting soule;
   	Sweet Spirit comfort me!

7. When the tapers now burne blew,
   And the comforters are few,
   And that number more then true;
   	Sweet Spirit comfort me!

8. When the Priest his last hath praid,
   And I nod to what is said,   30
   'Cause my speech is now decaid;
       Sweet Spirit comfort me!

9. When (God knowes) I'm tost about,
   Either with despaire, or doubt;
   Yet before the glasse be out,
       Sweet Spirit comfort me!

10. When the Tempter me pursu'th
    With the sins of all my youth,
    And halfe damns me with untruth;
        Sweet Spirit comfort me!   40

11. When the flames and hellish cries
    Fright mine eares, and fright mine eyes,
    And all terrors me surprize;
        Sweet Spirit comfort me!

12. When the Judgment is reveal'd,
    And that open'd which was seal'd,
    When to Thee I have appeal'd;
        Sweet Spirit comfort me!

A Thanksgiving to God, for his House

Lord, Thou hast given me a cell
        Wherein to dwell;
And little house, whose humble Roof
        Is weather-proof;
Under the sparres of which I lie
        Both soft, and drie;
Where Thou my chamber for to ward
        Hast set a Guard
Of harmlesse thoughts, to watch and keep
        Me, while I sleep.   10
Low is my porch, as is my Fate,
        Both void of state;

And yet the threshold of my doore
      Is worn by'th poore,
Who thither come, and freely get
      Good words, or meat:
Like as my Parlour, so my Hall
      And Kitchin's small:
A little Butterie, and therein
      A little Byn,   20
Which keeps my little loafe of Bread
      Unchipt, unflead:
Some brittle sticks of Thorne or Briar
      Make me a fire,
Close by whose living coale I sit,
      And glow like it.
Lord, I confesse too, when I dine,
      The Pulse is Thine,
And all those other Bits, that bee
      There plac'd by Thee;   30
The Worts, the Purslain, and the Messe
      Of Water-cresse,
Which of Thy kindnesse Thou hast sent;
      And my content
Makes those, and my beloved Beet,
      To be more sweet.
'Tis thou that crown'st my glittering Hearth
      With guiltlesse mirth;
And giv'st me Wassaile Bowles to drink,
      Spic'd to the brink.   40
Lord, 'tis thy plenty-dropping hand,
      That soiles my land;
And giv'st me, for my Bushell sowne,
      Twice ten for one:
Thou mak'st my teeming Hen to lay
      Her egg each day:
Besides my healthfull Ewes to beare
      Me twins each yeare:
The while the conduits of my Kine
      Run Creame, (for Wine.)   50
All these, and better Thou dost send
      Me, to this end,

That I should render, for my part,
    A thankfull heart;
Which, fir'd with incense, I resigne,
    As wholly Thine;
But the acceptance, that must be,
    My Christ, by Thee.

To his Conscience

Can I not sin, but thou wilt be
My private *Protonotarie*?
Can I not wooe thee to passe by
A short and sweet iniquity?
I'le cast a mist and cloud, upon
My delicate transgression,
So utter dark, as that no eye
Shall see the hug'd impietie:
Gifts blind the wise, and bribes do please,
And winde all other witnesses: 10
And wilt not thou, with gold, be ti'd
To lay thy pen and ink aside?
That in the mirk and tonguelesse night,
Wanton I may, and thou not write?
It will not be: And, therefore, now,
For times to come, I'le make this Vow,
From aberrations to live free;
So I'le not feare the Judge, or thee.

Another Grace for a Child

Here a little child I stand,
Heaving up my either hand;
Cold as Paddocks though they be,
Here I lift them up to Thee,
For a Benizon to fall
On our meat, and on us all. *Amen.*

A Christmas Caroll, sung to the King in the Presence at White-Hall

CHOR. What sweeter musick can we bring,
        Then a Caroll, for to sing
        The Birth of this our heavenly King?
        Awake the Voice! Awake the String!
        Heart, Eare, and Eye, and every thing
        Awake! the while the active Finger
        Runs division with the Singer.

FROM THE FLOURISH THEY CAME TO THE SONG.

1 Dark and dull night, flie hence away,
  And give the honour to this Day,
  That sees *December* turn'd to *May*.   10

2 If we may ask the reason, say;
  The why, and wherefore all things here
  Seem like the Spring-time of the yeere?

3 Why do's the chilling Winters morne
  Smile, like a field beset with corne?
  Or smell, like to a Meade new-shorne,
  Thus, on the sudden? 4. Come and see
  The cause, why things thus fragrant be:
  'Tis He is borne, whose quickning Birth
  Gives life and luster, publike mirth,   20
  To Heaven, and the under-Earth.

CHOR. We see Him come, and know him ours,
        Who, with His Sun-shine, and His showers,
        Turnes all the patient ground to flowers.

1 The Darling of the world is come,
  And fit it is, we finde a roome
  To welcome Him. 2. The nobler part
  Of all the house here, is the heart,

CHOR. Which we will give Him; and bequeath

This Hollie, and this Ivie Wreath,   30
To do Him honour; who's our King,
And Lord of all this Revelling.

THE MUSICALL PART WAS COMPOSED BY
M. HENRY LAWES.

The Widdowes teares: or, Dirge of Dorcas

1. Come pitie us, all ye, who see
   Our Harps hung on the Willow-tree:
   Come pitie us, ye Passers by,
   Who see, or heare poor Widdowes crie:
   Come pitie us; and bring your eares,
   And eyes, to pitie Widdowes teares.
       CHOR. And when you are come hither;
               Then we will keep
               A Fast, and weep
               Our eyes out all together.   10

2. For *Tabitha*, who dead lies here,
   Clean washt, and laid out for the Beere;
   O modest Matrons, weep and waile!
   For now the Corne and Wine must faile:
   The Basket and the Bynn of Bread,
   Wherewith so many soules were fed
       CHOR. Stand empty here for ever:
               And ah! the Poore,
               At thy worne Doore,
               Shall be releeved never.   20

3. Woe worth the Time, woe worth the day,
   That reav'd us of thee *Tabitha!*
   For we have lost, with thee, the Meale,
   The Bits, the Morsells, and the deale
   Of gentle Paste, and yeelding Dow,
   That Thou on Widdowes didst bestow.

[*The Widdowes teares: or, Dirge of Dorcas*]   146

CHOR. All's gone, and Death hath taken
    Away from us
    Our Maundie; thus,
    Thy Widdowes stand forsaken.   30

4. Ah *Dorcas, Dorcas!* now adieu
  We bid the Creuse and Pannier too:
  I and the flesh, for and the fish,
  Dol'd to us in That Lordly dish.
  We take our leaves now of the Loome,
  From whence the house-wives cloth did come:
    CHOR. The web affords now nothing;
      Thou being dead,
      The woosted thred
      Is cut, that made us clothing.   40

5. Farewell the Flax and Reaming wooll,
  With which thy house was plentifull.
  Farewell the Coats, the Garments, and
  The Sheets, the Rugs, made by thy hand.
  Farewell thy Fier and thy Light,
  That ne're went out by Day or Night:
    CHOR. No, or thy zeale so speedy,
      That found a way
      By peep of day,
      To feed and cloth the Needy.   50

6. But, ah, alas! the Almond Bough,
  And Olive Branch is wither'd now.
  The Wine Presse now is ta'ne from us,
  The Saffron and the Calamus.
  The Spice and Spiknard hence is gone,
  The Storax and the Cynamon,
    CHOR. The Caroll of our gladnesse
      Ha's taken wing,
      And our late spring
      Of mirth is turn'd to sadnesse.   60

7. How wise wast thou in all thy waies!
  How worthy of respect and praise!

How Matron-like didst thou go drest!
How soberly above the rest
Of those that prank it with their Plumes;
And jet it with their choice purfumes.
   CHOR. Thy vestures were not flowing:
           Nor did the street
           Accuse thy feet
        Of mincing in their going.   70

8. And though thou here li'st dead, we see
A deale of beauty yet in thee.
How sweetly shewes thy smiling face,
Thy lips with all diffused grace!
Thy hands (though cold) yet spotlesse, white,
And comely as the Chrysolite.
   CHOR. Thy belly like a hill is,
           Or as a neat
           Cleane heap of wheat,
        All set about with Lillies.   80

9. Sleep with thy beauties here, while we
Will shew these garments made by thee;
These were the Coats, in these are read
The monuments of *Dorcas* dead.
These were thy Acts, and thou shalt have
These hung, as honours o're thy Grave,
   CHOR. And after us (distressed)
           Sho'd fame be dumb;
           Thy very Tomb
        Would cry out, *Thou art blessed.*   90

The white Island: or place of the Blest

In this world (the *Isle of Dreames*)
While we sit by sorrowes streames,
Teares and terrors are our theames
        Reciting:

But when once from hence we flie,
More and more approaching nigh
Unto young Eternitie
                    Uniting:

In that *whiter Island*, where
Things are evermore sincere;   10
Candor here, and lustre there
                    Delighting:

There no monstrous fancies shall
Out of hell an horrour call,
To create (or cause at all)
                    Affrighting.

There in calm and cooling sleep
We our eyes shall never steep;
But eternall watch shall keep,
                    Attending   20

Pleasures, such as shall pursue
Me immortaliz'd, and you;
And fresh joyes, as never too
                    Have ending.

His Meditation upon Death

Be those few hours, which I have yet to spend,
Blest with the Meditation of my end:
Though they be few in number, I'm content;
If otherwise, I stand indifferent:
Nor makes it matter, *Nestors* yeers to tell,
If man lives long, and if he live not well.
A multitude of dayes still heaped on,
Seldome brings order, but confusion.
Might I make choice, long life sho'd be with-stood;
Nor wo'd I care how short it were, if good: 10

Which to effect, let ev'ry passing Bell
Possesse my thoughts, next comes my dolefull knell:
And when the night perswades me to my bed,
I'le thinke I'm going to be buried:
So shall the Blankets which come over me,
Present those Turfs, which once must cover me:
And with as firme behaviour I will meet
The sheet I sleep in, as my Winding-sheet.
When sleep shall bath his body in mine eyes,
I will believe, that then my body dies: 20
And if I chance to wake, and rise thereon,
I'le have in mind my Resurrection,
Which must produce me to that *Gen'rall Doome*,
To which the Pesant, so the Prince must come,
To heare the Judge give sentence on the Throne,
Without the least hope of affection.
Teares, at that day, shall make but weake defence;
When Hell and Horrour fright the Conscience.
Let me, though late, yet at the last, begin
To shun the least Temptation to a sin; 30
Though to be tempted be no sin, untill
Man to th'alluring object gives his will.
Such let my life assure me, when my breath
Goes theeving from me, I am safe in death;
Which is the height of comfort, when I fall,
I rise triumphant in my Funerall.

This Crosse-Tree here
Doth   JESUS   beare,
Who sweet'ned first,
The   Death   accurs't.

Here all things ready are, make hast, make hast away;
For, long this work wil be, & very short this Day.
Why then, go on to act: Here's wonders to be done,
Before the last least sand of Thy ninth houre be run;
Or e're dark Clouds do dull, or dead the Mid-dayes Sun.

   Act when Thou wilt,   10
   Bloud will be spilt;
   Pure Balm, that shall
   Bring Health to All.
   Why   then,   Begin
   To   powre   first   in
   Some Drops of Wine,
   In   stead   of   Brine,
   To search the Wound,
   So   long   unsound:
   And, when that's   20
   done, Let Oyle, next,
   run, To cure the Sore
   Sinne   made   before.
   And O! Deare Christ,
   E'en   as   Thou   di'st,
   Look down, and see
   Us   weepe   for   Thee.
   And tho (Love knows)
   Thy   dreadfull   Woes
   Wee   cannot   ease;   30
   Yet doe Thou please,
   Who   Mercie   art,
   T'accept each Heart,
   That   gladly   would
   Helpe, if it could.
   Meane while, let mee,
   Beneath   this   Tree,
   This   Honour   have,
   To make my grave.

Notes

"HESPERIDES

The name was applied not only to the daughters of Hesperus but also to their garden in the Fortunate Isles at the western extremity of the earth. See *O.E.D. s.v.*, I. c. Herrick implies that his poems, fruits of the west country, are to be associated with the golden apples which the mythical garden contained. For other possible associations see a note by G. C. Moore Smith in *Mod. Lang. Rev.* ix, July 1914, pp. 373-4." (L. C. Martin's note.)

THE ARGUMENT OF HIS BOOK
3: *Hock-carts:* last carts in from the harvest. 3: *Wassails:* merry gatherings.

WHEN HE WOULD HAVE HIS VERSES READ
8: *A round, A round:* a call to dance a round. 10: *Cato:* any severe critic.

THE PARLIAMENT OF ROSES TO JULIA
5: *State:* a canopy of state.

LOVE'S PLAY AT PUSH-PIN
Push-pin: a child's game played by pushing pins alternately.

TO HIS MISTRESSES
4: *Nectarell:* Herrick's coined adjective meaning nectarlike.

ALL THINGS DECAY AND DIE
3: *Lusters:* from L. *lustrum*, a period of five years.

TO THE KING

1644, when most of the West was in the hands of King Charles. See Marchette Chute, ch. 25, pp. 235 ff. 11: *White Omens:* favorable omens.

TO THE REVEREND SHADE OF HIS RELIGIOUS FATHER

Herrick was only a year old when his father died in 1592. See Chronology, page 29.

TO DEAN-BOURN

12: *Salvages:* savages.

BARLY-BREAK: OR, LAST IN HELL

Barly-break: a country game resembling prisoners' base; *hell* was the middle-ground in which the catchers stood.

A COUNTRY LIFE

24: *Brasse:* money (slang). 26: *Cocker:* pamper. 27: *Tearcely:* tersely, purely. 30: *Neat:* dainty, elegant, tasteful. 113: *Colworts:* cabbages. 117: *Size:* "assize, a fixed allowance of food, a ration" (Pollard).

TO THE PAINTER

2: *Bice:* Brownish gray. 10: *Burling iron:* pincers for removing burls (pimples) from the face.

UPON CUFFE

2: *Briefs:* "Letters-patent or licence for a collection for some charitable object" (Grosart).

UPON SCOBBLE

Scobble: Scobell is a Devonshire name that appears in the Dean Prior Register. See Grosart, Memorial introduction, on Devonshire names introduced by Herrick in his epigrams.

HIS FARE-WELL TO SACK

4-5: *Life / To quick action:* There have been several different interpretations of these lines. It appears to me that Herrick is saying that "sack is as dear to me as blood is to life, and nearer to me than life itself is to 'quick action' or to the Bride's 'warm soft side.'"

"Herrick persists (with a shrewdness worthy of Sir James Frazer) in seeing the May-day rites as religious rites, though, of course, those of a pagan religion. The flowers, like worshipers, bow to the east; the birds sing 'Mattens' and 'Hymnes'; and the village itself, bedecked with greenery, becomes a cluster of pagan temples. . . . Corinna is actually being reproached for being late to church—the church of nature . . . the street itself turns into a park, and the boys and girls returning with their arms loaded with branches of white-thorn, merge into the plants themselves. Corinna, like them, is subject to nature, and to the claims of nature; and the season of springtime cannot, and ought not, to be denied" (Cleanth Brooks). See Mr. Brooks's complete discussion of the poem, *The Well Wrought Urn*, pp. 62-73. 2: *God unshorne:* Apollo, with his unshorn *(intonsi)* locks. "In Herrick's poem, 'the god unshorne' is obviously the prepotent bridegroom of nature, the fertility god himself, toward whom the plants bow in adoration and whose day is now to be celebrated" (Brooks, *op. cit.*, p. 73). 13: *When as:* when. 25: *Titan:* the sun. 28: *Beads:* prayers.

AN ODE TO MASTER ENDYMION PORTER
Herrick is here referring, as in the following poem, to the death of his own brother William. See Marchette Chute, *op. cit.*, pp. 199-200. 20: *Mar'l:* marvel.

ON GELLI-FLOWERS BEGOTTEN
Gelli-flowers: gillyflowers.

UPON SOME WOMEN
3: *Thrumme:* odds and ends of thread. 8: *Sceanes:* scenes, coverings.

THE WELCOME TO SACK
7: *Convinces:* overcomes.

UPON GUBBS
1: *Kitlings:* kittens.

TO LIVE MERRILY
7: *Pap:* sap. 10: *Arabian dew:* spikenard. 12: *Re-*

torted: thrown back. 22: *Ovid . . . one Nose:* a play on the name Ovidius *Naso.* 25: *Immensive:* measureless. 28: *Terce:* terse.

TO THE VIRGINS, TO MAKE MUCH OF TIME
"The attic-like quality of Herrick's mind may have been one reason why he was so devoted to Robert Burton, whose *Anatomy of Melancholy* was now in its fifth edition. . . . Burton collected, for instance, the remarks of a great many authors on the subject of virgins and roses and the evanescence of youth. Herrick took the miscellaneous heap and gave them perfect shape . . ." (Marchette Chute, *op. cit.,* p. 249).

TO THE LARK
2: *Mattens:* matins.

THE FAIRIE TEMPLE
On the subject of Herrick's fairy poems, see Pollard, vol. 2, p. 306. *Mr. John Merrifield, Counsellor at Law:* All Herrick's fairy poems are dedicated to lawyers, and some names are probably invented. Grosart suggests that "Merrifield" may be "Merry Field." 10: *Halcion:* kingfisher. 17: *Neech:* niche. 22: *Idol-Canker:* worm. 26: *Cornish:* cornice. 34: *Saint Tit, Saint Nit,* etc.: "Tit" and "Nit," along with other such obviously made up names, are to be found in Drayton's *Nymphidia.* The names here are intended to suggest ancient saints. 35: *Mab's-state:* Queen Mab's chair of state. 64: *Bruckel'd:* begrimed. 65: *Cockall:* cockal, knuckle-bones. 67: *Codlin:* codling, a kind of apple. 74: *Fetuous:* featous, well-formed, elegant. 79: *Watched:* watchet, light blue, sky blue. 84: *I:* Aye. 101: *Bent:* blade of coarse grass. 121: *Nits:* nuts. 137: *Lady of the Lobster:* "The calcareous structure in the stomach of a lobster, serving for the trituration of its food; fancifully supposed to resemble the outline of a seated female figure" (O.E.D.). 139: *Chives of Saffron:* the yellow stamens of crocuses. 143: *Shed:* cocoon.

TO MUSIQUE, TO BECALME HIS FEVER
26: *Baptime:* baptism.

UPON HIMSELFE
1: *Mop-ey'd:* short-sighted.

DRAW GLOVES
Draw Gloves: an old game played by seeing which player can most quickly draw off a pair of gloves.

THE HOCK-CART, OR HARVEST HOME
9: *Maukin:* malkin, a cloth. 20: *Prank:* adorn. 21: *Crosse the Fill-horse:* bestride the shaft-horse. 34: *Frumentie:* frumenty, wheat boiled in milk and seasoned with cinnamon and sugar. 40: *Fanes:* fans. 40: *Fatts:* vats. 45: *Neat:* oxen.

UPON GROYNES
2: *Holy-Forum:* churchyard. 2: *Candidate:* in a white sheet, doing penance.

THE POETS GOOD WISHES
The Duke of Yorke: afterwards James II.

A NUPTIALL SONG, OR EPITHALAMIE
8: *Tiffanie:* gauze. 36: *More disparkling:* throwing off more sparks in different directions. 61: *Codled:* literally, boiled. 84: *Lace:* a girdle. 114: *Brusle:* bristle, raise its feathers.

THE SILKEN SNAKE
See Introduction, pages 20-21.

OBERONS FEAST
1: *Shapcot:* Thomas Shapcott, a Devonshire lawyer friend of Herrick's, to whom he dedicated two poems describing the court of the fairies. 24: *Kitling eyes:* green, like a kitten's. 29: *Fuz-ball:* Puff-ball. 33: *Sagge:* heavy.

THE KISSE
9: *Babies of the eyes:* the small image of oneself reflected in the pupil of another's eye.

CHOP-CHERRY
Chop-cherry: bob-cherry, a children's game.

UPON HIS KINSWOMAN MISTRIS ELIZABETH HERRICK
Elizabeth, Herrick's niece, daughter of William Herrick, died in 1630 at the age of eleven.

TO HIS NEPHEW
2: *Urbin:* Raphael. 2: *Tintarret:* Tintoretto. 3: *Brugel:* Breugel. 3: *Coxie:* Michael van Coxcie, Flemish painter.

TO DIANEME
6: *Assention:* ascension.

THE MAD MAIDS SONG
Swinburne said of this poem that it "can only be compared with Blake's, which has more of passionate imagination if less of pathetic sincerity."

OBERONS PALACE
6: *Mickle:* much. 14: *Carries Hay in's horne: foenum habet in cornu*, is dangerous. 17: *Peltish:* angry. 26: *Redeem:* probably regain. 28: *Lemster Ore:* Leominster wool. 37: *Ceston:* cestus. 48: *Picks:* diamonds on playing cards. 51: *Counter:* "counters such as are used in gambling, and dice with their pips (or eyes) worn off" (Grosart). 75: *Corrupted:* phosphorescent. 83: *Errours:* wanderings. 98: *Comply:* embrace. 101: *Spinner:* spider.

TO OENONE
The simplicity and grace of these stanzas, according to Swinburne, recall the Restoration lyrists "in their cleanlier and happier mood."

HIS WINDING-SHEET
47: *Platonick yeere:* a cycle in which the heavenly bodies were supposed to go through all their possible movements and return to their original relative positions.

TO PHILLIS TO LOVE, AND LIVE WITH HIM
19: *Carkanets:* carcanets, necklaces. 30: *The Heyes:* a winding country dance.

HIS CONTENT IN THE COUNTRY
4: *Prew:* his servant, Prudence Baldwin.

THE APPARITION OF HIS MISTRESSE

1: *Desunt nonnulla:* "something is wanting," to justify perhaps the abruptness of the opening. 15: *Purfling the Margents:* embroidering the borders. 32: *Linus:* a mythical poet. 41: *Comply:* encircle. 54: *Evadne:* in *The Maid's Tragedy*. In an earlier version of the poem Shakespeare's name appears in place of Beaumont's, and there is no reference to the heroine of *The Maid's Tragedy*, which was probably first performed in 1611. Herrick's change reflects the shift in popular taste.

THE BAD SEASON MAKES THE POET SAD

14: *Knock at a Starre:* from Horace (*sublimi feriam sidera vertice*).

THE NIGHT-PIECE, TO JULIA

The meter of this poem is the same as the song in Jonson's *The Gypsies Metamorphos'd*, beginning "The faery beam upon you."

THE BEGGAR TO MAB, THE FAIRIE QUEEN

7: *Souce:* salt-pickle. 11: *Huckson:* hockshin, the underside of the thigh. 13: *Chit:* shoot, sprout. 19: *Orts:* scraps.

THE COUNTRY LIFE

22: *Soyl'd:* manured. 57: *Fox i'th'Hole:* a boy's game in which they lift up one leg and hop on the other. 58: *Mummeries:* performances by mummers, or disguised actors. 66: *Cockrood:* a road or run for snaring woodcocks. 76: *Cætera desunt:* "the rest is wanting."

UPON HIS VERSES

5: *Toucht:* stamped.

THE FUNERALL RITES OF THE ROSE

See William Empson, *Seven Types of Ambiguity*, p. 162. 10: *Trentall:* a service for the dead.

NOT EVERY DAY FIT FOR VERSE

4: *Fantastick Pannicles:* cells of the brain in which fancy is bred.

10: *Creeking*: creaking, cackling. 24: *Miching*: thieving, pilfering.

A TERNARIE OF LITTLES
Pipkin: a small earthenware pot.

THE WAKE
8: *Marian*: Maid Marian of the Robin Hood ballads. 14: *Incurious*: easily pleased, uncritical.

A HYMNE TO BACCHUS
22: *George-a-Green*: a legendary rustic hero celebrated in the anonymous comedy, *George a Green, Pinner of Wakefield*.

UPON JULIA'S CLOTHES
See Introduction, pages 21-23.

KISSES LOATHSOME
6: *Wimbling*: "boring, hole-making" (Martin). 7: *Pokingsticks*: "used for stiffening the plaits of ruffs" (Martin).

THE VISION
9: *Cull'd*: embraced. 10: *Cup-shot*: drunken.

HIS DESIRE
6: *Citterne*: cithern, a sort of guitar. 6: *Quill*: plectrum for playing the cithern.

THE PILLAR OF FAME
The last line is from Ovid: *Vita verecunda est, Musa jocosa, mihi.*

HIS NOBLE NUMBERS

HIS LETANIE, TO THE HOLY SPIRIT
13: *Artlesse*: unskillful.

A THANKSGIVING TO GOD, FOR HIS HOUSE
22: *Unflead*: unflayed, unskinned.

TO HIS CONSCIENCE
2: *Protonotarie*: court clerk. 8: *Hug'd*: hugged.

ANOTHER GRACE FOR A CHILD
3: *Paddocks:* frogs.

THE WIDOWES TEARES
41: *Reaming:* drawing out into threads.

THE WHITE ISLAND
11: *Candor:* whiteness.